THE GOAL BEHIND THE GOAL

Uncovering & Transforming The hidden
Saboteur Limiting Your Success

BY MONA THORPE

Copyright © 2025 by Mona Thorpe
The Goal Behind the Goal: Uncovering & Transforming The Hidden Saboteur Limiting Your Success

All rights reserved. No part of this publication may be reproduced, stored in a retrieval system, or transmitted in any form or by any means—electronic, mechanical, photocopying, recording, or otherwise—without the prior written permission of the publisher, except in the case of brief quotations used in reviews, articles, or academic references.

This book is intended for informational and educational purposes only. The author and publisher are not engaged in rendering psychological, legal, financial, or medical advice. Readers are encouraged to consult appropriate professionals for personal guidance.

Published by Success 411 Publishing
www.success411.com

First Edition: 2025

For more resources, programs, or support, visit:
www.success-411.com

PREFACE

We've all been there—doing the "right" things, setting goals, repeating affirmations, visualizing outcomes. And yet... something doesn't click. Success stays one step out of reach. If that sounds familiar, you're not alone—and you're not broken. There's a deeper reason, and it's not laziness, lack of willpower, or not "wanting it enough." It's misalignment.

This book is the result of decades of work helping people transform their goals into reality—not through hype, but through clarity. What I've discovered is that most people don't fail because they're not trying. They fail because they're unknowingly operating with two goals: one conscious, one hidden. One says yes. One says no. And until those two goals get on the same page, no amount of action will fully get you there.

This book will guide you in identifying that hidden goal—your inner saboteur—and showing you how to shift it. You'll learn how to align your inner world with your desired outcomes. When that happens, success stops being a chase... and starts becoming natural.

TABLE OF CONTENTS

PREFACE III

INTRODUCTION: The Real Reason You Feel Limited 1

CHAPTER 1: The Illusion of Forward Motion 5

CHAPTER 2: Understanding the Hidden Goal 13

CHAPTER 3: How Saboteur Goals Are Formed 29

CHAPTER 4: Signs You're Out of Alignment 41

CHAPTER 5: When Positive Thinking Isn't Enough 47

CHAPTER 6: The Power of Competing Intentions 57

CHAPTER 7: Identifying Your Hidden Driver 63

CHAPTER 8: Why Willpower Fails 67

CHAPTER 9: Uncovering Core Misbeliefs 71

CHAPTER 10: The Alignment Method – Step by Step 77

CHAPTER 11: Realigning Thought and Emotion 83

CHAPTER 12: Rewriting the Internal Contract 91

CHAPTER 13: Building Success from the Inside Out 97

CHAPTER 14: Living in Alignment..101

CHAPTER 15: You Had the Power All Along...............................107

CHAPTER 16: How to Recognize the Hidden Goal That's Still Running the Show 113

CHAPTER 17: Life After the Shift 181

A DAY IN LIFE AFTER THE SHIFT.. 189

CHAPTER 18: Triggers, Tests & Transformation 193

CHAPTER 19: Your Success Set Point — And How to Raise It... 203

CHAPTER 20: Seeing the Invisible — Understanding Others Through the Lens of Hidden Patterns.. 209

CONCLUSION: Walking Forward with Clarity 221

YOU DON'T HAVE TO DO THIS ALONE 223

ABOUT THE AUTHOR 225

ACKNOWLEDGMENTS..227

INTRODUCTION

THE REAL REASON YOU FEEL LIMITED

Let's be honest. The self-help aisle is crowded. Everywhere you turn, there's a new formula promising to help you get what you want: more money, better relationships, perfect health, peace of mind. You may have tried several of them. Maybe even all of them. And still, you're not where you thought you'd be.

This book doesn't come with flashing promises or limited-time bonuses. You won't find countdown clocks or "one-time offers." What you will find is truth—perhaps uncomfortable at times but liberating.

Because here's the reality: You've likely been working against yourself without realizing it. You've been setting conscious goals while carrying subconscious ones that contradict them. These common hidden messages from childhood often shape our adult behaviors and sound like:

- "Don't be too much."
- "If I shine, I'll be rejected."
- "I have to struggle to be worthy."
- "I must take care of everyone else before myself."

- "It's safer to play dumb."
- "If I speak up, I'll be punished."
- "Being different is dangerous."
- "Keep the peace, even if it means losing yourself."
- "If I succeed, they'll hate me."
- "Don't be happier than your parents."
- "If I'm not needed, I'll be abandoned."
- "Never need anything — or they'll control you."
- "Love always comes with a cost."
- "I'm only valuable if I'm suffering."
- "If I relax, it'll all fall apart."
- "I have to stay small to stay safe."
- "If I outgrow them, I'll be alone."
- "I must earn love by being useful."
- "I'm only lovable when I'm struggling."
- "Joy makes me a target."
- "Don't get your hopes up — it'll only hurt."
- "Trusting people is stupid."
- "No one really wants the real me."
- "If I win, they lose — and that's not allowed."
- "Too much success means something bad will happen."
- "Stay invisible — it keeps you safe."
- "If I stop proving myself, I'll disappear."
- "If I shine too brightly, someone will take it away."
- "Success will cost me love."

They don't show up as thoughts. They show up as friction. As self-doubt. As procrastination. As endless preparation and little to no action. You don't lack motivation. You're just internally misaligned.

This book isn't about forcing success. It's about making it frictionless by resolving the tug-of-war within you. We'll explore how competing goals are formed, how to identify yours, and most importantly—how to align your inner world with what you truly want.

Once that happens, the blocks and limitations fall away. The over-efforting stops. And success—real, sustainable, joyful success—begins.

CHAPTER 1

THE ILLUSION OF FORWARD MOTION

You've got the planner. You've got the vision board. Maybe even the mastermind group and the highlighters in three colors. You're listening to podcasts on the drive to work, reading the right books, and doing your best to think positively, heck you are thinking positively!

But underneath all that activity, there's a quiet question growing louder:

WHY AM I NOT FURTHER ALONG?

This is the illusion of forward motion. It feels like progress. It looks like momentum. But deep down, something isn't moving. You know it. You feel it.

This illusion is especially tricky because it's socially rewarded. People admire discipline, people who "do the work." But real change doesn't come from surface effort alone. It comes from **alignment**.

Imagine trying to row a boat with one oar going forward and the other backward. That's what happens when your conscious goal and subconscious beliefs aren't on the same team. You row and row, but you stay in circles. You exhaust yourself and blame the wind. Or worse—you blame yourself.

We live in a culture that praises hustle, but **hustling in the wrong direction is just a faster path to frustration.** Activity without clarity becomes its own trap. You might even feel ashamed to admit you're stuck, because everything around you says, "Just push harder. Just think more positively. Just keep going."

But here's the truth no one likes to say out loud: ***you can be moving—and still be stuck.***

That kind of being stuck doesn't come from lack of effort. ***It comes from contradiction.*** When two parts of your mind are working against each other, no affirmation, planner, or productivity hack will break you free. You're not blocked because you're lazy. You're blocked because something deeper inside you is saying, "No."

That "no" often is not heard by your hearing. It's experienced as a feeling of frustration and the inner unconscious words might be:

"I want it... but I can't" — Hidden Inner Conflicts:

- "I want success... but I don't want people to resent me."
- "I want wealth... but I'm afraid it will make me selfish."
- "I want to speak up... but I don't want to rock the boat."
- "I want a loving relationship... but I'm afraid I'll lose myself."
- "I want to be seen... but I don't want to be misunderstood."
- "I want to be powerful... but I'm afraid of becoming like them."
- "I want to feel free... but I don't want to be alone."
- "I want to rest... but I'm afraid I'll fall behind."

- "I want to take up space... but I don't want to make anyone uncomfortable."
- "I want to lead... but I don't want to be blamed."
- "I want to grow... but I don't want to leave anyone behind."
- "I want to be the best... but I don't want anyone to feel small."
- "I want joy... but I don't want to lose control."
- "I want to express myself... but I don't want to be judged."
- "I want peace... but I don't want to let my guard down."
- "I want more... but I don't want to seem ungrateful."
- "I want to take risks... but I don't want to disappoint anyone."
- "I want to expand... but I don't want to threaten the people I love."
- "I want to shine... but I don't want to trigger jealousy."
- "I want to win... but I don't want others to feel like losers."

Each of these inner conflicts forms what I call a **Trojan Goal—a hidden agenda** rooted in fear, guilt, or outdated survival patterns that overrides your higher ambitions. It's not sabotage. It's protection. But that protection has a cost.

Think of your goal like a GPS destination. You've set the address consciously. But if your subconscious doesn't believe the destination is safe or allowed, it will keep rerouting you.

You might:
- Start strong and fizzle out.
- Stay busy without gaining traction.
- Hit the same wall in different forms.
- Blame circumstances, other people—or yourself.

You've probably said things like:

- "Maybe I'm just not cut out for this."
- "I need more discipline."
- "I'll try harder next time."

But the truth is, you don't need more force.

You need more **alignment**.

When your conscious goal and your subconscious drivers are in sync, things start working. Momentum returns. Resistance drops. You're no longer dragging an anchor behind your boat. Instead, the wind is at your back—and this time, it's your own breath pushing you forward.

This illusion of forward motion is seductive. It gives you *'the high'* of productivity without the results of progress. It gives your ego a sense of "doing something," while your deeper self quietly waits for permission to lead.

So how do you know if you're in this illusion?

Here are a few signs:

- You're constantly learning but rarely applying.
- You're exhausted, but nothing big has shifted.
- You're trying several things at once, just in case.
- You're always planning, never launching.
- You keep getting ready to get ready.

You're always revising but never releasing.

- You have multiple half-finished projects, but few completions.

- You keep researching "just a little more" before starting.
- You've mapped out the next 10 steps but haven't taken the first.
- You spend hours tweaking the logo, the tagline, the playlist — but not the message.
- You're jumping from coach to coach, course to course — but not implementing.
- You constantly switch strategies before one has time to work.
- You talk about your goals more than you act on them.
- You're endlessly waiting for the "perfect timing" or "right feeling."
- You've made a to-do list for your to-do list.
- You feel a burst of momentum after organizing... but it fades fast.
- You avoid visibility tasks (posting, pitching, promoting) by working "behind the scenes."
- You keep setting new intentions but not following through on old ones.
- You convince yourself you're "not ready yet" — even though you know more than enough.
- You reframe old fears as "intuition" — when they're really resistance in disguise.
- You invest in learning or tools to feel in motion — but don't leverage them.
- You're waiting to feel confident before you begin... instead of building confidence by beginning.

Any Sound familiar? If so, don't panic. Don't judge yourself. Just see it for what it is: **a system glitch**, not a personal failure.

Before we dive into identifying the hidden saboteur, I want you to pause and ask yourself:

- What am I doing out of fear instead of desire?
- Who would I be if my success didn't scare me?
- Where in my life am I working hard and still not seeing results?
- Where do I keep starting over — and why?
- What am I doing out of fear instead of genuine desire?
- What "truth" about myself do I keep repeating that might not be true at all?
- What am I avoiding — not because I can't do it, but because it changes the way I'm seen?
- What would happen if I really let go of who I had to be growing up?
- Am I afraid of losing anyone if I become fully empowered?
- What do I believe success will cost me?
- Is there a hidden "benefit" to staying stuck — like staying connected to someone or something?
- How would I behave today if I didn't believe my past defined me?
- Where do I feel tension or resistance in my body when I think about success?

These questions aren't designed to make you uncomfortable. They're here to make you honest. Because honesty—not hype—is the first step to transformation.

You are not your patterns. You are not your failures. And you are not stuck because you lack effort or talent. You're stuck because a part of you is still trying to protect something it thinks you're not ready to lose.

And here's the irony: once you see it, you've already started to heal it.

The rest of this book will walk you through the process of uncovering, understanding, and transforming the hidden goal that's been quietly steering your ship.

This work is simple, but not always easy. It's not about willpower. It's about clarity. It's not about forcing results. It's about transforming resistance. And it begins with the courage to admit:

What I'm doing isn't working.

Not because I'm broken—

but because I'm in conflict.

You **don't need more motivation**. You need **more internal unity**.

In the next chapter, we'll explore what this hidden goal really is, how it got there—and how to begin taking your power back.

But for now, take a breath.

You've been trying harder.

Now it's time to work smarter.

Welcome to the start of your journey.

CHAPTER 2

UNDERSTANDING THE HIDDEN GOAL

If you've ever wondered, "Why do I keep getting in my own way?"—you're not alone.

The real answer isn't lack of willpower, laziness, or a flaw in your character. It's not even bad luck. More often than not, it's the result of a goal you don't even realize you've set.

This chapter is about that hidden goal—the one quietly running in the background of your mind, often with more power than the goal you consciously set.

Let's be clear: this isn't a woo-woo idea. This is neuroscience. Your subconscious runs about 90–95% of your daily behavior. It's not a villain, but it **is programmed** for safety, not success. And if success feels threatening, unfamiliar, or emotionally unsafe, your subconscious will steer you elsewhere—without asking for permission.

That subconscious "steering" is often invisible. Which is why, despite all your conscious focus on the life you want, you may feel like you're driving with one foot on the gas and one on the brake.

This inner friction can be subtle. You might be moving forward in your career but still procrastinating on applying for the role you really want. You might be in a relationship but unconsciously sabotaging its growth. You might say you want financial freedom but continue to overspend or undercharge.

Why?

Because behind your stated goal, there's **another goal**—one that's not about thriving but about surviving. And this goal is what we call **the hidden saboteur.**

Here's a personal example of how a hidden goal can sabotage and operate — not in theory, but in real life.

Many years ago, I started a mail-order business built around a charming plush cat — about 17 inches tall that I designed. It came with outfits for all occasions: Christmas, Halloween, birthdays, Thanksgiving, and more. My goal was simple: create a gift that would bring joy and lighthearted connection to whoever received it.

There were many moving parts, and I worked hard. A prototype had to be designed, manufacturing had to be arranged overseas (with the endless paperwork that comes with it), and distribution needed to be mapped out. Most importantly, I needed investors.

And I got them.

A group of investors came forward and offered to fund the business with $3 million. They had marketing power behind them, and they had just helped another product launch — which eventually sold for $11 million. The same potential existed for my company. On paper, it was a dream scenario.

And yet... I pulled out of the deal.

At the time, I told myself it wasn't fair — that something just didn't feel right. But a few months later, after deep personal reflection, I saw the truth. The deal had actually been incredibly generous.

So why did I sabotage it?

Because I had never known what it felt like to be a multi-millionaire. To be seen in that way. To receive abundance on that level. Deep inside, a hidden part of me felt unsafe.

You see, growing up, even small successes were met with emotional and physical torment. If I stood out, I was punished. If I shined, I was made to feel ashamed. My subconscious, always trying to protect me, developed a core pattern:

Lay low. Don't succeed. Don't be noticed. Stay safe. This pattern was unknown in my conscious mind.

And that pattern didn't vanish with age.

When the opportunity to become a millionaire showed up, that old programming kicked in... and took the wheel.

The **subconscious doesn't track time.** It operates through emotional memory and survival logic. To it, success **wasn't exciting — it was dangerous.**

Realizing this was a major turning point in my life — and an expensive one!

But it opened my eyes to just how powerful, and deeply embedded, these hidden goals can be. They're not always loud. Often, they show up as gut feelings, or "rational" decisions that make perfect sense in the moment — until you look back and see the truth.

The consequences of being unaware can be massive.

But awareness changes everything.

REFLECTION PROMPTS:

Spotting Your Hidden Pattern

Take a moment to sit with these questions. Let them guide you beneath the surface — not to blame or criticize, but to gently reveal what may be running the show behind the scenes.

- Have I ever walked away from a promising opportunity — and later wondered why?
- Did I ever *almost* succeed, only to hit an unexpected wall I couldn't explain?
- What feelings come up when I imagine myself being highly successful, visible, or wealthy?
- What messages did I receive growing up about people who had money, ambition, or success?
- Was there a time when standing out — even in a good way — led to punishment, shame, or disapproval?
- What did I *learn* (even without realizing it) about what was "safe" or "acceptable" for someone like me?
- Could I be playing small to stay connected to people I love — or to avoid outshining them?
- Is it possible that a younger version of me still believes that success = danger?

Journaling Tip: Don't try to get the "right" answers. Let your pen move. Let the truth emerge without pressure. Sometimes a single sentence reveals a pattern you've carried for decades.

WHAT IS A HIDDEN GOAL?

A hidden goal is an unconscious emotional aim designed to preserve something you associate with safety, identity, or belonging.

It may look like:
- Avoiding judgment
- Avoiding failure
- Avoiding attention
- Staying connected to family patterns
- Staying "good" or likable
- Maintaining a sense of control
- Avoiding responsibility
- Avoiding emotional risk
- Keeping others comfortable
- Not outshining a parent or sibling
- Never being "too much" for others
- Protecting yourself from abandonment
- Hiding talents to avoid triggering jealousy
- Repeating familiar roles (caretaker, underachiever, rebel, peacemaker)
- Staying quiet to avoid conflict
- Proving your worth through struggle
- Minimizing success to feel "normal"
- Keeping your dreams small to avoid disappointment
- Staying invisible so others don't feel threatened
- Holding yourself back to stay emotionally loyal to someone who didn't have the same chance

Let's say you want to be wealthy or achieve your next level of wealth. That's a clear conscious goal. But if subconsciously you've been programmed to believe "rich people are selfish" or "money ruins relationships," "I don't deserve success," "That's an unfamiliar place" then a hidden goal to *stay good* or *stay loved* might override your conscious intention.

That contradiction creates the tug-of-war: one part of you says go, another says no. This may not be the one you operate under but there are thousands of conflicting goals that work on sabotaging our conscious goals.

This isn't just theoretical—it's how the mind protects you. The subconscious isn't trying to ruin your life. It's trying to **keep you safe based on old programming.** But when that programming is based on outdated or false assumptions, it backfires.

The Origin of the Hidden Goal: More Real-Life Examples

- Maybe you watched a sibling get criticized for "showing off" — and learned to hide your talents so you wouldn't be next.

- Maybe your parents worked endlessly and were never home — and your subconscious equated ambition with abandonment.

- Maybe every time you expressed a big dream, someone laughed, rolled their eyes, or told you to be "realistic" — and you learned that dreaming big wasn't safe.

- Maybe you got more love when you were struggling than when you were succeeding — and success now feels like emotional isolation.

- Maybe your family valued toughness and stoicism — and any vulnerability was seen as weakness. So now, asking for help feels like a threat to your identity.

- Maybe you were the caretaker in a chaotic household — and you learned that your worth came from making others okay, not thriving on your own.

- Maybe you were always told "you're too sensitive" — so now you avoid attention because it makes you feel exposed or wrong for simply feeling deeply.
- Maybe success in your culture, household, or community was only acceptable in certain forms — and what you want doesn't fit that mold, so you self-sabotage.
- Maybe a moment of joy was always followed by criticism or punishment — so part of you believes happiness comes with a price.
- Maybe you were taught that being different, creative, or expressive was "weird" — and now authenticity feels unsafe, even though you crave it.

A clients came to me frustrated after being passed over for multiple promotions. While she eventually completed her tasks, it always required extraordinary effort. Her desk was perpetually cluttered, her work disorganized, and her small apartment mirrored the same chaos. Despite her desire to change and her repeated attempts to bring order into her life, nothing seemed to stick. No matter how hard she tried, she kept reverting to disarray — until we uncovered the *goal behind the goal*.

Through deeper exploration, she recalled her childhood vividly. Her father, a stern and demanding man with a military background, had strict expectations around order and discipline. He often criticized her for having a messy room or looking unkempt. Strikingly, she realized that when she tried to clean up and impress him, her efforts went unnoticed. But when she was messy — when she fell short — she received attention, even if it was critical. That negative attention became her only form of connection.

Unconsciously, her subconscious had made a powerful association: *being messy meant being seen*. It wasn't just a bad habit — it was a hidden strategy for staying emotionally tethered to a parent who rarely acknowledged her otherwise. Once she saw this pattern clearly, she was able to release it. No longer needing to sabotage herself to feel connected, she began cultivating a sense of love and validation in healthy, constructive ways.

This is a powerful example of how a hidden goal forms beneath the surface — often rooted in childhood — and continues to drive behavior long after the original situation has passed. These subconscious patterns, once protective, become hardwired until we consciously rewrite them.

As you can see, hidden goals rarely arise from logic — **they're built from emotion, repetition, and the deep human need to belong**. They don't announce themselves with fanfare. **They live in our reactions, our habits, our resistance, and the decisions we can't explain**. The good news? Once seen, they lose their power. **Awareness turns the unconscious into choice — and from choice, freedom is born.**

REFLECTION: SPOTTING THE ORIGINS OF YOUR HIDDEN GOAL

Take a few quiet moments and consider the following questions. Don't rush — you're not looking for perfect answers, just honest ones. You may be surprised at what surfaces when you give your subconscious a voice.

1. What behaviors or traits were rewarded in your childhood? Which ones were discouraged or punished?
    - Were you praised for being helpful? Quiet? Tough?
    - Were you criticized for being ambitious, sensitive, or expressive?

2. Who did you feel safest around growing up — and what did you have to do or be to keep that connection?
   - Did you have to dim yourself?
   - Did you take care of others emotionally or physically?
   - Did you learn that struggle earned love?

3. Was there a person in your life who was "too much" or "not enough" in the eyes of others?
   - Did you model yourself to avoid becoming like them?
   - Did you adopt traits just to be accepted or avoid rejection?

4. When you think about reaching your next level of success… what quiet discomfort shows up?
   - Does it feel unsafe to be seen?
   - Does part of you worry you'll lose people?
   - Does success feel lonely, greedy, or selfish?

5. If a younger version of you were watching you now, what would they be afraid of you becoming?
   - Someone too visible?
   - Someone too different from the family?
   - Someone too happy?

Whatever the origin, the subconscious sets a rule: *This keeps us safe.*

And the **subconscious mind, being brilliant at pattern recognition**, reinforces that rule every time something remotely similar happens.

It goes like this:

- You share an exciting new idea → a sibling says, "Don't get your hopes up" → your subconscious logs: "Ambition = disappointment. Stay small."
- You speak up at a meeting → someone interrupts or dismisses you → your subconscious logs: "Using my voice = being shut down. Stay silent."
- You buy something nice for yourself → someone makes a comment about being "wasteful" → your subconscious logs: "Having nice things = guilt. Don't receive."
- You win an award → a friend withdraws or seems envious → your subconscious logs: "Achievement = abandonment. Don't shine."
- You express confidence or pride → someone calls you "arrogant" → your subconscious logs: "Confidence = rejection. Stay humble, stay invisible."
- You try to rest or take a break → you're called "lazy" → your subconscious logs: "Rest = danger. Keep proving your worth."
- You say "no" to something draining → someone accuses you of being selfish → your subconscious logs: "Boundaries = rejection. Keep pleasing."
- You share something vulnerable → it's used against you later → your subconscious logs: "Authenticity = betrayal. Keep the mask on."
- You apply for a big opportunity → someone rolls their eyes → your subconscious logs: "Visibility = rejection. Better hide."
- You raise your rates → a client leaves → your subconscious logs: "Success = loss. Better undercharge."

- You try dating again → it ends → subconscious: "Love = pain. Stay single."

One event is enough to create a rule. Repetition solidifies it. And if never challenged, *it becomes a hidden goal that shapes your life silently.*

THE POWER OF COMPETING INTENTIONS

Let's take this deeper.

You've probably heard of the concept of limiting beliefs. They're the ideas like "I'm not enough" or "People like me don't succeed." Those beliefs are real and powerful—but they're only part of the story.

Because behind every limiting belief is an **adaptive strategy**—a behavior pattern meant to keep you safe, loved, or in control.

That strategy becomes a kind of unspoken goal.

Here's the key difference:

- **Conscious goal:** What you say you want
- **Hidden goal:** What your subconscious is programmed to protect you from.

And when those two goals are at odds, *the subconscious usually wins.*

Not because it's stronger, but because it's faster, quieter, and more deeply wired.

You don't even realize it's working against your efforts… until you see the pattern.

THE HIDDEN GOAL IN ACTION

Let's look at a real-world example.

Janet wants to build a coaching business. She's smart, trained, and has a network. But she keeps "waiting for the right time." She tweaks her website endlessly, rewrites her bio, and takes another course instead of marketing her business.

Her conscious goal? Build the business.

But her hidden goal? Avoid rejection.

She grew up with emotionally distant parents who criticized her whenever she spoke up. Speaking now—being visible, asking for money, owning her expertise—feels dangerous to her nervous system.

So, *her subconscious* **creates delays that feel like preparation but are actually procrastination dressed in productivity.**

Until Janet identifies that hidden goal, she'll keep circling instead of launching.

IT'S NOT SELF-SABOTAGE. IT'S MISALIGNED SAFETY.

One of the biggest shifts you can make is this:

Stop calling it self-sabotage. Start calling it **misaligned safety**.

Your subconscious is not your enemy. It's your bodyguard. But it's been operating off old files—***often ones you didn't even write***.

Once you start identifying the emotional payoffs of staying stuck, you stop feeling like a failure—and start getting curious.

Ask yourself:

- What am I afraid will happen if I succeed?
- What would I have to give up to get what I want?
- Who might I outgrow if I achieve my goal?
- What does staying stuck allow me to avoid?
- What am I afraid will happen if I succeed?
- What would I have to give up to get what I want?
- Who might I outshine, upset, or outgrow if I achieve this goal?
- What does staying stuck allow me to avoid?
- What role have I taken on to feel loved, safe, or needed?
- Who am I protecting by staying where I am?
- What fear would success force me to face?
- What discomfort does failure help me delay?
- What version of me might no longer belong if I change too much?

These questions are not about guilt—they're about awareness. Awareness brings choice. **And choice is the beginning of power.**

Sometimes, staying stuck protects you from confronting grief, guilt, rejection, disconnection, or visibility. These aren't failures. They're emotional logic loops you can now gently unravel — not by force, but with compassionate understanding.

Your job isn't to push through the resistance. It's to listen to what it's trying to preserve... and then remind it: you're safe now. You get to choose a new path.

SHINING A LIGHT ON THE INVISIBLE

The Pause That Changes Everything

One of the most powerful practices you can use on this journey is learning to **pause when you feel resistance.**

Not to shame it. Not to push through it. But to **get curious.**

In that pause, ask yourself:

"**What am I protecting right now?**"

It's not always fear of failure or success. Those are symptoms. The **deeper truth is: you're trying to protect something.**

It may appear on the outside to be the below but follow it down the rabbit hole and seek to find what is below the surface of these.

- **Your reputation** — "If I try and fail, I'll look foolish."
- **Your comfort** — "If I take this risk, everything could change too fast."
- **A relationship** — "If I grow, will they still accept me?"
- **An old identity** — "Who am I without the role I've always played?"
- **Family loyalty** — "No one else in my family did this. Who do I think I am?"
- **Predictability** — "At least I know how to manage where I am now."
- **Familiar struggle** — "If I stop struggling, will I lose my purpose?"
- **Control** — "What if I get what I want and still don't feel good enough?"
- **Invisibility** — "If I succeed, I'll have to be seen… and judged."

- **Resentment** — "If I move forward, I can't keep blaming others."
- **Connection** — "If I outgrow this, who will I still belong with?"

Often, the very thing we're protecting is the thing that is **quietly keeping us small** — not because it's wrong, but because it no longer fits who we're becoming.

This kind of resistance doesn't mean you're broken.

It means a **part of you still thinks the old identity is your best chance at love, safety, or inclusion.** But you now know something more:

You're allowed to keep growing — even if it shakes things up.

You're allowed to be successful, visible, happy — even if others choose not to follow.

You're allowed to release what once protected you, so you can step into what now *reflects you*.

And it all starts in the pause.

FROM CONFLICT TO CLARITY

The good news is that once you see the hidden goal, you can work with it—not against it.

You can negotiate. Reframe. Update. Align.

You don't have to wrestle with yourself anymore. You can thank the old strategy for keeping you safe, then give yourself permission to choose a new one.

This **doesn't happen overnight. But the shift from confusion to clarity happens the moment you see the tug-of-war for what it is.**

You don't have to force your goals into existence. You just have to stop blocking them.

And that begins **with awareness.**

REFLECTION: GETTING HONEST ABOUT YOUR HIDDEN GOAL

Take a few quiet moments to reflect on the following:

- What do I say I want?
- What patterns show up when I try to pursue it?
- What fear or story might be running beneath the surface?
- What hidden payoff am I still protecting?

Let your answers surprise you. Let them teach you something new about yourself. **Don't worry about "fixing" anything yet. This chapter is about illumination**.

In the next chapter, we'll dive into **how these hidden goals are formed—and why it's not your fault**. You'll begin to see how your mind was trained, and how to start **retraining it to align with the life you really want.**

For now, take a breath.

You've been driven by a hidden goal.

Now it's time to bring it into the light.

CHAPTER 3

HOW SABOTEUR GOALS ARE FORMED

*"You weren't born to sabotage yourself.
You were trained to survive — and you got really good at it."*

It starts early. Long before you knew how to spell "goal," you were already forming one: Stay safe. Stay accepted. Stay connected.

Maybe you became the overachiever. Or the peacemaker. Or the quiet one who never needed much. These weren't random traits — they were strategies. You didn't choose them. You adapted to them. Because at some point, your brain received a signal: this is how I keep love, or this is how I avoid pain, or this is how I stay connected.

And that signal became your subconscious navigation system.

You didn't consciously set a hidden goal to stay invisible, to undercharge, or to stall your own progress. But your nervous system did. It happened while you were still learning how the world worked. You **gathered emotional data from the faces of your caregivers, the tone of their voices, the patterns of approval and withdrawal.**

Children don't have critical thinking. They have absorption. What's repeated becomes truth. What's rewarded becomes identity.

In the next chapter, we'll look at how these hidden goals show up in your adult life — through hesitation, disconnection, over-efforting, and more.

You'll learn to spot the signs that you're out of alignment and begin making powerful course corrections.

Because once you understand where the misalignment began, you can stop rowing in circles — and start sailing in the direction you were always meant to go.

Let's pause here to illustrate just how powerful these hidden saboteur goals can be—and why their grip doesn't disappear in adulthood.

THE ASTRONAUT ANALOGY: A FEAR THAT NEVER GREW UP

Imagine you're an astronaut. You're snug and safe inside a spaceship, floating with your fellow astronauts through space. There's warmth, companionship, conversation, food when you're hungry, and water when you're thirsty. Everything you need is inside. **You feel protected but must important connected.**

But something outside the ship needs repair, and you're the one suited-up to fix it. You step out, tethered to the ship with a safety rope. **You still feel secure—until the unthinkable happens: the rope breaks.**

Suddenly, you're drifting into the vast, empty silence of space. You watch the ship and your crew growing smaller in the distance. The people who made you feel safe, the environment that sustained you—they're fading from view. Panic rises. **You're not just physically detached, you're 'existentially' alone** aimlessly floating in an empty abyss of darkness.

This isn't just about being far from others. It's about **complete severance from your source of connection and survival.**

This is the emotional equivalent of what a young child feels when their connection to a caregiver is threatened. To a child, disapproval, rejection, or abandonment isn't discomfort—it's annihilation. **We are biologically wired to associate emotional connection with life itself.**

That terror, once embedded in our subconscious, doesn't simply evaporate as we age. It **hides under adult responsibilities, achievements, and logic—but it's still there, quietly steering choices.**

So when we grow up and sense that success, authenticity, or self-expression might risk disapproval, **that ancient panic gets triggered. We may not be floating into space, but we do float away from what we believe are sustaining our life.**

This isn't irrational—it's ancient wiring.

Tribal cultures once used this wiring intentionally. On some islands, disobedient tribe members were sailed off and left on deserted shores—cut off from community, from life. It was the ultimate punishment. Not because they'd lose physical comfort, but **because they'd lose 'belonging'.**

Your inner saboteur uses the same logic.

Better stay small than risk exile. Better delay than stand out. Better obey the old rules than question them and drift into an abyss of aloneness.

But here's the **good news: the rope didn't break. You're no longer a child. And what once protected you no longer has to confine you.**

Understanding this fear is the first step in releasing its grip—and writing a new contract with your mind.

WHY IT'S NOT YOUR FAULT

This is one of the most important things I can say to you in this book:

You are not broken.

You are patterned.

The **"you" that doubts, hesitates, or fears success isn't flawed — it's trained.** You didn't design the training. **You adapted to it in order to survive and belong. That's not sabotage. That's brilliance.**

But brilliance misdirected becomes a trap.

What once kept you safe can now keep you stuck.

The problem is, you may not even recognize it as a problem — because it's always been your normal.

THE HIDDEN CONTRACT

Imagine a child who grows up hearing things like:

- "Be grateful for what you have."
- "That dream is too big for someone like you."
- "Don't make waves."
- "You're too sensitive."
- "You're getting a little too full of yourself."
- "We're not the kind of people who…"
- "Don't ask for too much."

- "Just be happy with your job and stop wanting more."
- "Act your place."
- "You're not the smart one in the family."
- "That kind of success changes people."
- "Don't show off — no one likes a show-off."
- "Stick with what's safe."
- "It's selfish to want more when others have less."
- "Who do you think you are?"
- "Life isn't about being happy — it's about surviving."

These kinds of phrases are often delivered casually, even lovingly — but they plant powerful subconscious messages.

REFLECTION: UNCOVERING THE MESSAGES YOU INHERITED

Take a quiet moment to reflect. The words and **energies you absorbed in childhood didn't just pass through you — they shaped you**. And they may still be whispering beneath your decisions today.

You don't need to blame anyone. This is not about judgment. It's about illumination. When you can **see what was planted, you gain the power to choose what grows.**

Ask yourself:

- **What were some of the *spoken* messages in my household about success, money, or self-worth?**
- (e.g., "Don't brag," "Money's tight," "You'll never be like them")

- **What were some of the *unspoken* messages?**
- *(Think: emotional reactions, facial expressions, silence when you expressed joy, discomfort when you shared dreams.)*
- **Were there things you learned were "too much" to want?**
- *(Too much attention, too much ambition, too much happiness?)*
- **What identity did you feel most accepted in?**
- *(Were you the helper? The quiet one? The tough one? The one who didn't need anything?)*
- **What did your caregivers or community seem to *value most*?**
- *(Was it humility? Loyalty? Sacrifice? Staying small? Being easy to deal with?)*
- **What parts of yourself did you feel you had to hide to stay loved or included?**

Write down anything that comes up — no matter how small or strange. Sometimes, the quietest comments hold the biggest clues.

And remember you're not doing this to relive the past. **You're doing this to reclaim the truth of who you are** — underneath the inherited programming.

That child absorbs not just messages, but **rules**.

And from those rules, they subconsciously sign an emotional contract:

- "If I stay small, I stay loved."
- "If I don't stand out, I won't be left."
- "If I don't ask for more, I'm safe."

Years later, that ***child becomes an adult who sets goals with one hand while holding themselves back with the other.***

They try to speak up — but their voice shakes.

They raise their prices — then immediately offer a discount.

They say they want love — but avoid vulnerability.

They don't know they're still living by rules they never chose.

THE ROOTS OF SABOTEUR GOALS

Hidden goals are built around emotional safety. They're shaped by a few core forces:

1. Fear of Loss

- "If I change, I'll lose connection."
- "If I succeed, people will resent me."
- "If I have more, I'll be alone."

2. Desire for Approval

- "If I'm successful, I'll be seen as arrogant."
- "If I'm different, I won't be accepted."
- "If I shine, I will lose friends."

3. Avoidance of Pain

- "Better to not try than to fail."
- "Success leads to burnout."
- "Visibility equals criticism."

4. Inherited Guilt
- "My parents struggled — who am I to thrive?"
- "My family didn't have this — I shouldn't either."
- "If I outgrow them, I'm betraying them."

Each of these emotional themes can anchor a powerful internal contract.

Until those contracts are examined — and consciously rewritten — they continue running the show, even when your outer life looks "successful."

COMMON HIDDEN GOAL TYPES

Let's break it down further with some real-world examples.

The Invisible Achiever

They hit goals but stay emotionally guarded. Their hidden goal?

Don't get too close — closeness isn't safe.

The Chronic Helper

They give endlessly but never ask for anything. Hidden goal?

Stay useful so no one leaves.

The Over Corrector

They micromanage and perfect everything. Hidden goal?

If I control enough, nothing will go wrong.

The Self-Doubter

They hide behind research, more credentials, or "just one more course."

Hidden goal? *If I stay in learning mode, I never have to risk being seen.*

These identities aren't weaknesses — they're defense systems. And they've been *working*... until now.

FAMILY SYSTEMS AND EMOTIONAL ROLES

In most families, unspoken emotional roles get assigned without anyone realizing it:

- The Responsible One
- The Irresponsible One
- The Caretaker
- The Smart One
- The Dumb One
- The Quiet One
- The One Who Causes No Trouble
- The One Always in Trouble
- The One Who Always Smiles
- The One Who Never Smiles

These **roles are often based on what the family needs you to be — *not who you truly are.***

And if "success" **threatens to disrupt that role, your subconscious will quietly pull you back in line.** Not out of cruelty. Out of emotional loyalty.

This is especially strong in families where struggle, sacrifice, or scarcity are seen as noble — and anything outside that narrative is viewed with suspicion.

CULTURE, RELIGION, AND IDENTITY SCRIPTS

Beyond family, we absorb beliefs from culture, religion, and social identity.

- "Good girls don't ask for more."
- "Men don't show emotion."
- "Success without suffering is unearned."
- "We don't talk about money."
- "Putting yourself first is selfish."

These become collective contracts — and breaking them can feel like betrayal, even when no one says so directly.

If you're carrying a belief that success must look a certain way — or that it comes with shame, punishment, or distance — you will subconsciously resist it. Or water it down. Or abandon it altogether.

Not because you lack desire. But because part of you believes the cost is too high.

THE NERVOUS SYSTEM CONNECTION

Let's zoom in on something deeper: the **body.**

Your nervous system doesn't know the difference between real danger and perceived emotional threat. To your brain, public speaking can feel as dangerous as a bear attack. Setting a boundary can feel like exile.

When your nervous system perceives a subconscious threat to your safety, it activates protective responses:

- Freeze (stalling, procrastinating)
- Fawn (people-pleasing, over-apologizing)

- Flight (changing goals frequently, ghosting)
- Fight (resisting feedback, self-criticism, perfectionism)

These aren't character flaws — they're physiological responses.

Until the subconscious sees success as safe, these patterns will persist.

WHY YOUR BRAIN CLINGS TO THE OLD

The subconscious prioritizes the **familiar**, not the functional.

Its primary job is to *keep things predictable*, because predictability feels safe.

So even if your old habits are sabotaging you, they're *familiar*.

That makes them "safe" in the brain's eyes.

New beliefs, even if better, feel dangerous at first. This is why people stay in bad relationships, unfulfilling jobs, or patterns they claim to hate.

To move forward, your brain has to *unlearn* the idea that comfort equals safety — and learn that *growth* can become safe, too.

That process starts with awareness.

YOUR OLD GOAL ONCE SAVED YOU

It may sound strange, but I invite you to thank your hidden goal.

At some point in your life, it served you:

- It kept you out of danger.
- It won you approval.

- It helped you navigate chaos.
- It gave you a sense of control.

But just like a **life jacket in shallow water eventually weighs you down,** your old strategy may now be the very thing drowning your success.

Let go of blame. Replace it with understanding.

Your hidden saboteur isn't an enemy. It's a strategy that's outlived its job.

REFLECTION PROMPTS

Take time with these. They are not surface questions.

- What patterns from childhood still echo in my life?
- What emotional rules did I absorb from my family or culture?
- What did I learn I had to be — in order to be loved or accepted?
- What part of me still believes success is unsafe?
- What "role" am I outgrowing?

Be honest. Be kind. This chapter is not about judgment. It's about beginning to see the architecture of your mindset — so you can rebuild it on your terms.

CHAPTER 4

SIGNS YOU'RE OUT OF ALIGNMENT

Alignment isn't just a feeling. It's a state of internal agreement. When your conscious goals and your subconscious beliefs are on the same page, progress feels natural. You make decisions with clarity, act with confidence, and navigate challenges with resilience.

But when you're out of alignment, life feels like a grind. You're pushing but not moving. Or worse, you're moving—but not in the direction you truly want to go.

Let's take a deeper look at how misalignment shows up in everyday life.

One of the most common signs is chronic procrastination. Not the occasional delay, but the recurring pattern of resistance when it comes to the things that matter most to you. This isn't laziness—it's inner conflict. Your **conscious mind says 'go,' but your subconscious whispers 'wait.'**

Maybe you keep putting off writing your book. Or launching that side business. Or having that important conversation. You know it matters. You even want it. But something invisible blocks your follow-through. That something is often a subconscious belief telling you it's not safe to proceed.

Another sign is burnout—not just physical fatigue, but emotional depletion. You feel like you're giving everything you've got, yet the return feels minimal. You might find yourself thinking, "Why am I working so hard and getting nowhere?" **This is a sign that you may be working against your own deeper wiring.**

People-pleasing is another subtle saboteur. You constantly say yes to others at the expense of your own needs. You bend, adjust, and suppress your voice to maintain harmony. Over time, this erodes self-trust and creates quiet resentment. You may be living a life that looks good on the outside but feels off on the inside.

Then there's perfectionism. A sneaky one. You delay launching your idea because it's not 'ready.' You rewrite the same paragraph ten times. You won't post your offer until every graphic is flawless. Underneath this desire for excellence is often a fear of judgment. If it's perfect, you won't be criticized. But if you never launch, you can't fail.

Chronic indecision is another red flag. When both options feel unsafe, the brain stalls. You spin in loops of overthinking. You poll ten friends. You delay, deflect, distract. The real fear isn't choosing wrong—it's choosing something that puts your subconscious identity at risk.

Even physical symptoms can be indicators. Do you get migraines every time you approach a new level in your business? Does your back ache when you're about to ask for a raise? Does your energy crash before a big presentation? **Your body is a messenger. It responds to subconscious stress, not just surface events.**

Misalignment also shows up in relationships. You attract partners who mirror your fears. You struggle to set boundaries. You hide your truth to avoid rocking the boat. **You may even sabotage intimacy because deep down, vulnerability feels dangerous.**

Financial patterns reveal a lot, too. **Maybe you make money but can't seem to keep it.** Or you undercharge and overdeliver. Or you fear success because of what you think it will cost you—relationships, freedom, peace. These are signs of a deeper inner script running the show.

Here's the truth: these patterns are not moral failings. They are survival strategies. They were formed to protect you at some earlier time. But they no longer serve who you're becoming.

Let's do a quick exercise to illuminate where you might be out of alignment. Grab a pen and write down one goal you've had for a while but haven't reached yet. Now list three reasons you think it hasn't happened. Be honest. Not polite. Then ask yourself: what fear is underneath each reason?

You might discover fears of judgment, loss, failure, exposure, or rejection. These fears often trace back to childhood, where pleasing others or staying small felt safer than standing out.

Misalignment isn't always dramatic. Sometimes it's subtle. A soft tension in your gut. A hesitancy in your voice. A dream that feels more exhausting than exciting. **These are not random—they are your compass.**

Pay attention. These cues are guidance. **Not to push harder, but to pause and realign.**

You don't need more hustle. You need more harmony between your head and your heart. **Your willpower won't win a war against your wiring. But alignment? That's where everything changes.**

In the next chapter, we'll talk about why positive thinking alone can't override these hidden blocks—and what to do instead.

Let's dig deeper into how misalignment appears in four of the most common life domains: career, relationships, finances, and health.

In career, misalignment can look like feeling overqualified and underpaid—because you hesitate to advocate for yourself. Or it shows up when you stay in a job that drains you, simply because pursuing your passion feels too risky. You might fear success as much as failure, because rising too far could threaten your identity, relationships, or sense of belonging.

Many high performers hit what looks like burnout, but what they're actually experiencing is misalignment fatigue. They've built success around an old story—the 'shoulds' they inherited rather than the vision they actually desire. Eventually, the dissonance between outer achievements and inner truth catches up, creating deep dissatisfaction.

In **relationships, misalignment** often shows up as shrinking your needs, deferring your desires, or dimming your voice. ***It's the partner who never fully shows up emotionally, but you stay—because part of you believes asking for more risks being left***. Or it's the dynamic where you become the caretaker, the fixer, or the pleaser, not because it's who you are, but because it's what once kept you safe.

These patterns may have helped you survive childhood, but they sabotage intimacy in adulthood. You begin to believe love means self-sacrifice. That connection requires compliance. And the hidden fear is: If I speak my truth, I'll end up alone.

Financial misalignment is also common. You may have a strong income goal, but undercharge or avoid raising your rates. Or you spend impulsively, not from joy, but from the emotional high of temporary relief. Or you never quite feel safe, no matter how much you save.

These patterns often stem from deep beliefs: that you're not worthy of more, that wealth makes you selfish, or that success will isolate you. Without realizing it, you sabotage the very abundance you crave.

Health is another mirror. You may intellectually want to be healthy, yet avoid sleep, binge on sugar, or ignore signs of stress. The disconnect isn't from ignorance—it's from an inner contract you haven't renegotiated. Maybe health feels like a burden. **Or being vibrant threatens your identity as someone who's always struggling.**

Now let's shift from observation to integration. Below are five reflection prompts designed to help you connect with your own signs of misalignment. Take your time with each one—your answers may surprise you:

1. What is one goal you've struggled to achieve, despite repeated effort? What does part of you 'gain' by not reaching it?
2. Where in your life do you feel frequent frustration or fatigue? What might that be signaling?
3. Are there goals you've 'put on hold' for years? What beliefs are keeping them paused?
4. When you think about getting what you truly want, what's the **first uncomfortable emotion that surfaces—guilt, fear, anxiety, disbelief?**

5. What roles or identities have you adopted (caretaker, overachiever, peacemaker) that might be at odds with the life you desire?

Use your answers not to shame yourself—but to understand yourself. **Self-awareness is the beginning of all transformation.**

Realignment doesn't happen through pressure. It begins with permission—the permission to want what you want without apology. The permission to question your internal contracts. The permission to rewrite them.

Here's something important to remember: **You're not behind. You're not broken. You're not late. You've simply been trying to run a race with one foot tied to an old belief.**

And now, you're untying the knot.

Alignment is not a finish line. It's a way of living. A way of relating to yourself with honesty, courage, and compassion.

It's the quiet knowing that your outer actions and inner truths are finally moving in the same direction.

In the next chapter, we'll explore one of the most common misconceptions in the self-development world—why positive thinking alone isn't enough to create lasting change, and how to build the emotional foundation for real transformation.

CHAPTER 5

WHEN POSITIVE THINKING ISN'T ENOUGH

Positive thinking is one of the most popular personal development tools in the world. It's optimistic. It's empowering. It's simple. And when you're in alignment, it's even effective.

But when your subconscious mind is holding onto old beliefs, unprocessed fears, or outdated internal contracts, positive thinking alone becomes like placing a fresh coat of paint over a cracked foundation. It may look good for a while, but eventually, the cracks show through.

Let's be clear: **positive thinking isn't the enemy. It's just incomplete.**

Imagine trying to **steer a ship using only a rudder, with no awareness of the underwater currents below.** You can point the vessel wherever you like, but if a powerful current is pulling in the opposite direction, the ship won't go where you intend. In the same way, your conscious thoughts are only part of what drives your behavior.

If your subconscious mind believes that success leads to disconnection, or that happiness invites jealousy, or that speaking up will get you hurt—*no amount of affirmations will override those inner contracts. Not until those contracts are revealed, understood, and rewritten.*

This is where many well-intentioned people get stuck. They do the vision boards, the morning mantras, the gratitude journals. They say all the right things, think all the right thoughts—*but nothing changes. It's not because they're doing it wrong. It's because they're only addressing the surface.*

Your subconscious is the emotional engine of your life. It responds not to what you want consciously, but to what you 'believe' unconsciously. And until the two are aligned, change feels hard—like trying to drive with the parking brake on.

Take a moment to reflect. Have you ever *repeated a positive affirmation—something like* "I am worthy" or "Money flows easily to me"—*only to feel a twinge of discomfort, doubt, or even emotional resistance?* That discomfort is your **inner system saying, "We don't believe this yet."**

Affirmations that conflict with inner beliefs don't create transformation. They create inner tension. And when we don't know how to resolve that tension, we either double down on the practice or abandon it altogether.

This is why so many people give up on self-help tools and especially those about the law of attraction. Not because the tools are broken, but because they were *applied without addressing the deeper layers.*

Here's what's missing: before affirmations can take root, the soil needs to be cleared. You can't grow flowers in a garden full of rocks and weeds. **The work of uncovering limiting beliefs, outdated**

fears, and subconscious patterns is the emotional gardening that makes space for new growth.

Let's look at a few examples:

- If you grew up in a household where money was scarce and associated with stress, no amount of repeating 'I am abundant' will override the imprint that wealth causes conflict.

- If you were taught to keep quiet to stay safe, repeating 'I speak my truth with confidence' may trigger anxiety—not because the phrase is wrong, but because it conflicts with a subconscious contract tied to survival.

- If you were conditioned to believe that love requires sacrifice, then 'I deserve a healthy relationship' might feel foreign—because it challenges the role you've unconsciously learned to play.

This is the crux of why positive thinking can't stand alone. It's a tool, not a transformation. True transformation happens when you align your conscious desires with your subconscious programming.

To do this, you must **be willing to go beneath the surface. To meet the part of you that's scared, guarded, or skeptical—not to silence it, but to understand it.**

When you bring **compassion to the parts of you that don't believe yet, something shifts. The resistance softens**. The inner system begins to rewire itself. And your affirmations move from empty words to embodied truths.

This **doesn't mean you stop using affirmations. It means you pair them with inner inquiry. With curiosity. With emotional honesty.** You make them an invitation, not an imposition.

Try this: Instead of saying, 'I am successful,' try asking, 'What part of me doesn't feel safe being successful?' Listen. Write. Explore. That's where the gold is.

This is not a quick fix. It's not always sexy. But it's real. And real creates results.

One of the most liberating shifts you can make is understanding that **discomfort doesn't mean you're broken—it means you're being honest. And honesty is the first step toward freedom.**

In the next chapter, we'll talk about the role of competing intentions—how your inner saboteur can be motivated by protection, not sabotage, and what to do about it.

Let's bring this into everyday life. Picture someone named Jim. He's been repeating his affirmations every morning: 'I am a confident leader. I speak up and take charge.' Yet in every meeting at work, he stays quiet, letting others take the lead. It's not that he lacks intelligence or skill—he's brilliant—but a deeper belief whispers, 'If I speak up, I'll be seen as arrogant. I'll lose approval. I'll be rejected.'

This internal contradiction creates emotional friction. While Jim's conscious self wants success, his subconscious self wants safety. And between the two, safety will always win—until he consciously realigns his system.

What's the antidote? First, awareness. Jim must notice the tension. Then, inquiry: Where did I learn that confidence equals arrogance? Who told me speaking up was dangerous? From there, he can begin to dismantle the old association and replace it with truth: I can be confident and kind. I can lead without losing love.

Another example: Marcus wants to start his own business. He's visualized it, affirmed it, even written the plan. But every time he gets close to launching, he self-sabotages. Misses deadlines. Avoids the final steps. Why? Because somewhere deep inside, Marcus believes success will make him less relatable to his friends and family. He's afraid of outgrowing the people he loves.

This is one of the most overlooked reasons people stay stuck—not fear of failure, but fear of change. Fear of leaving others behind. **Fear that success means disconnection. And positive thinking won't touch that kind of fear unless it's brought to light and rewritten.**

So how do we go deeper? How do we use these signs as signals instead of setbacks?

We start by creating space—not just physical space, but emotional space. Stillness. Reflection. We listen to the parts of ourselves that have been trying to protect us from harm, even if their methods no longer serve us.

We pair affirmations with questions. **We honor our desires without overriding our fears. We acknowledge that part of growth means grieving old identities and outdated roles.**

Try adding these prompts to your affirmation practice:

- What part of me isn't ready for this change?
- What belief does this affirmation challenge?
- If this affirmation became true, what would I have to let go of?

These questions don't weaken your progress—they strengthen it. They build the bridge between what you say and what you believe. And that bridge is the birthplace of real change.

There is no shame in resistance. It's often the sign of something sacred inside you that wants to be acknowledged. When you meet it with curiosity instead of criticism, you create space for alignment.

So yes, keep the affirmations. But make them conversations. Make them invitations. Let them be less about forcing change and more about understanding your inner terrain.

Because when you do that—when your affirmations grow roots in self-awareness and compassion—they stop being scripts and start becoming truths. And from there, everything begins to shift.

The most powerful belief is the one your whole system agrees with. That's the real power of alignment.

Let's go further and explore how positive thinking, when misapplied, can unintentionally invalidate real emotional experiences. Consider someone going through grief, trauma recovery, or a major life transition. Being told to simply 'stay positive' can feel dismissive rather than supportive. It's not encouragement—it's erasure.

This creates a silent emotional burden where individuals begin to feel guilty for feeling anything other than optimistic. **They suppress their sadness, their confusion, their real-time processing of pain—all in an attempt to be what they think 'growth' should look like.** But ignoring emotion isn't growth. It's postponement.

True alignment doesn't mean you only feel positive emotions. It means you **trust yourself enough to feel them all—and still stay aligned with your vision. Positive thinking has its place, but emotional literacy must come first. Without it, we're building skyscrapers on sand.**

We must become fluent in our emotional signals. **Every emotion, even the uncomfortable ones, holds information.** Anxiety might mean you're out of integrity. Anger could signal a crossed boundary. Sadness may invite reflection and reevaluation. These aren't signs of failure—they're invitations for reconnection.

When you skip past your emotional reality, you miss the moment when transformation is actually possible. That's why skipping to positive thinking too soon can be like turning the page before finishing the paragraph—you miss the message.

Think of your psyche like a negotiation table. Your conscious mind shows up like the enthusiastic executive with the vision board and quarterly goals. But across the table sits your subconscious, holding all the budget approvals, past data, and risk assessments. If those two aren't in agreement, the deal doesn't move forward.

You can't bully your subconscious into alignment. You can't outthink its objections. You have to invite it into the conversation—and give it a voice. **What does it need? What does it fear? What is it protecting? When you build this dialogue, you build real momentum.**

Let's talk about timeline pressure. Many people combine positive thinking with strict time frames—'I will achieve X by the end of the year.' And while clarity and deadlines can create structure, when your subconscious doesn't believe the goal is safe or achievable, the deadline becomes a source of shame rather than motivation.

This is why self-sabotage is often misdiagnosed. What looks like procrastination is often protection. What looks like laziness is often a lack of alignment. Before you set another timeline, check in with the part of you that needs reassurance—not just the part that wants results.

Here's a journal prompt that can shift your entire perspective: **'What part of me feels threatened by this goal becoming real?' Sit with it. Write from that voice. Let it speak, without judgment.** What you discover may surprise you—and free you.

Let's not forget cultural and societal overlays. Many of us are raised in systems that reward overworking, perfectionism, and appearance over authenticity. In that context, positive thinking can become another mask—another tool for pretending everything's fine when you're barely holding it together.

When we try to bypass our inner complexity with surface-level optimism, we rob ourselves of wholeness. And wholeness, not perfection, is what creates sustainable success.

Instead of trying to override our discomfort, we can choose to integrate it. We can make room at the table for both hope and fear, ambition and doubt, movement and rest. **When all parts are welcome, resistance fades. You don't have to fight yourself anymore.**

This is the heart of alignment: building a relationship with your inner world where honesty replaces performance. Where progress becomes a conversation, not a command. **Where success arises not from forcing your way forward but from removing what holds you back.**

Let's reframe positive thinking as a tool for amplification—not substitution. It works best when it amplifies truth, not when it attempts to override reality. **When your affirmations are rooted in awareness, they become resonant. When they're layered over avoidance, they lose their power.**

Incorporating emotional congruence into your self-talk changes the game. Try saying: **'Even though part of me is afraid, I'm willing to grow.' Or: 'It's safe to take one small step, even if I'm not fully confident yet.**' These statements build bridges. They honor where you are while pointing toward where you want to go.

Another helpful shift: anchor your affirmations in action. *Instead of just saying, 'I am disciplined,' pair it with: 'Today, I'll complete one task that reflects my focus.' Action validates the belief.* It gives your subconscious evidence. And over time, belief and behavior fall into sync.

Lastly, remember this: you are not behind. There's no scoreboard for inner work. No finish line to rush toward. *Alignment isn't about arriving. It's about evolving. And every time you pause to listen, question, feel, and choose consciously—you're already doing the work that matters most.*

In the next chapter, we'll look at how these inner conflicts show up as competing intentions—and why what looks like sabotage is often just protection in disguise.

CHAPTER 6

THE POWER OF COMPETING INTENTIONS

Let's revisit the metaphor of the inner rowing team—your conscious mind paddling toward your stated goal, while your subconscious paddles toward emotional safety. If these rowers are not moving in unison, it doesn't matter how strong your intentions are—you'll end up going in circles. That's exactly what happens when competing intentions are left unresolved.

This rowing team analogy becomes even more powerful when we realize that each 'rower' may be carrying the weight of past experience. One may have internalized childhood rejection, another is trying to manage the fear of success, and yet another fears the loss of approval from loved ones. **None of them are bad—they're just carrying unprocessed emotion.**

Here's the critical insight: alignment isn't about getting rid of these parts of yourself. It's about unifying them under a shared goal. This requires deep listening, trust, and conscious integration.

Let's take a real-world example: a woman named Alisha wants to expand her coaching business. She's brilliant, experienced, and deeply committed. But she finds herself hesitating when it's time to post content or promote her services. She tells herself she's 'just being humble'—but the truth is deeper. Through reflection, Alisha realizes she fears being judged as inauthentic or arrogant—just like her mother once accused her of when she shared her achievements as a child.

This competing intention is driven by a subconscious contract: 'If I stay quiet and small, I stay safe and loved.' But staying small is killing her dreams. Once Alisha becomes aware of this internal agreement, she can begin rewriting it. Her new truth becomes: 'I can be visible and remain authentic. I can grow and still be loved.'

We all carry subconscious contracts like this—beliefs formed in our early years that once helped us survive but now limit us. Bringing them to light allows us to revise them. That's when traction begins.

It's worth noting that sometimes your **competing intentions aren't rooted in fear—they're rooted in identity.** If you've always seen yourself as 'the reliable one,' then launching a bold new venture may feel threatening because it clashes with how you believe others see you. The subconscious voice says, 'Who will I be if I change?'

That's why resolving these inner conflicts isn't just about goal-setting—*it's about identity evolution. It's about allowing yourself to outgrow the story you've lived inside of, especially when that story has kept you stuck.*

So, how do you begin dissolving these conflicting patterns? Here's a three-step process you can try:

1. **Reveal the Fear** – Ask yourself: What's the worst-case scenario if I succeed? What does part of me fear I'll lose or threaten by moving forward?
2. **Validate the Emotion** – Don't judge the fear. Honor it. Say: 'I see you. I understand you're trying to protect me.'

3. **Rewire the Intention** – Introduce a new belief that meets the same need but supports your growth. Example: 'I can grow without losing love. I can succeed and remain grounded.'

Let's pause here for a metaphor: Your conscious goal is the GPS destination. But your subconscious is the driver. If they disagree on where to go, you won't get anywhere. Real success happens when **both the destination and the driver agree—it's safe to proceed.**

Another analogy: think of your mind like a symphony. Each instrument represents a desire, belief, or fear. If one section is playing a different tune, it creates dissonance. Image what it would sound like with the different sections playing different songs. It would sound like a bunch of screeching sounds. Alignment means tuning the whole orchestra—*not silencing parts but harmonizing them.*

This is also why people sometimes manifest partial success. They reach a goal but don't feel fulfilled—or they lose it quickly afterward. *It's not because they were undeserving. It's because part of them wasn't fully on board. Competing intentions quietly unraveled what they worked to build.*

The good news? Awareness changes everything. *Once you identify a competing intention, it loses its invisibility. You can work with it, dialogue with it, and evolve it.*

Try this journaling prompt: 'If I were afraid to succeed, what would that fear be trying to protect me from?' Let your hand write whatever comes. Don't edit. You might be surprised at the honesty and wisdom that emerge.

One more story: Jason wanted to propose to his partner. Everything in his life was ready—finances, love, timing. But he kept hesitating.

When asked why, he stated, 'I'm not sure.' After a guided session, he realized that growing up, he saw his father lose his identity in marriage. His subconscious was screaming, 'Don't lose yourself.' Once he understood this, Jason can affirm a new truth: 'Partnership can amplify who I am—not erase me.'

These moments of insight don't just shift your thinking—they unlock action. They unfreeze progress. Because when your whole self is in agreement, there's nothing pulling you backward.

Competing intentions aren't roadblocks. They're opportunities to become whole. To know yourself more deeply. To become a creator rather than a reactor.

So, ask yourself: Where might my foot be on the gas and the brake at the same time? And more importantly—what conversation needs to happen inside me to move forward in unity?

Let's look at a classic internal conflict: the desire for freedom versus the desire for security. Many people say they want the freedom to travel, work on their own terms, or express themselves more openly. But a hidden competing intention says, 'If I do that, I might lose the stability I need to feel safe.' This creates a silent tug-of-war that paralyzes action. You may find yourself 'trying' to create freedom while clinging tightly to the very structures that limit it.

This dynamic plays out in relationships too. Someone may long for deep connection and emotional intimacy—but recoil when it begins to form. Why? Because another intention is at play: 'If I get too close, I could get hurt.' Again, not sabotage—just an outdated script that hasn't been consciously rewritten.

Your internal guidance system works much like a GPS. But if there are two destinations plugged in simultaneously—say, 'thrive' and 'stay safe'—your internal system goes haywire. You don't get very far before hitting a loop of indecision, false starts, or backtracking.

One of the most overlooked signs of a competing intention is chronic indecision. When you can't make a choice or constantly revisit old decisions, it's often a sign that multiple internal goals are clashing below the surface. It's not that you're incapable of deciding— *it's that each path threatens a different value or belief you hold. Once those values are surfaced, decision-making becomes much clearer.*

People sometimes believe they are lazy or lack discipline, when in reality, they're exhausted from the inner resistance caused by unrecognized competing intentions. It's not a flaw in motivation— it's a misalignment of inner drivers. When you resolve the conflict, energy returns. Clarity returns. And so does momentum.

A helpful question to ask yourself regularly is: 'Is this hesitation about capacity… or about inner conflict?' You may find that what you've labeled as procrastination is actually your **subconscious waving a red flag trying to protect you. But if you spot this you can help your subconscious by pausing and realigning.**

Here's a practical strategy for handling competing intentions: create a 'goal dialogue.' Write out your conscious goal on one side of a paper. On the other side, write the fears, objections, or concerns that arise. Then let them speak to each other. What do they need? What do they fear? What new agreement could you offer that integrates both perspectives?

This exercise may sound abstract, but it's grounded in neuroscience. Dialoguing with your inner parts allows you to shift the emotional and neurological associations tied to a goal. It creates neural flexibility and opens the door to integration, which is the real foundation of lasting change.

The bottom line is this: you don't have to get rid of any part of you to succeed. You only need to get every part working together. This is the essence of alignment. And it's the opposite of pushing, striving, or forcing. Alignment feels lighter, smoother, and—ironically—more powerful than sheer effort ever could.

As we move forward, remember this: **every time you feel stuck, consider that a part of you might simply be waiting to be heard. And once it is, your energy is no longer split. You are free to move—fully, completely, and with grace.**

CHAPTER 7

IDENTIFYING YOUR HIDDEN DRIVER

Let's take a moment to consider how insidious these hidden drivers can be—*not because they are malicious, but because they operate silently.* They rarely speak in full sentences. Instead, they emerge as hesitation, procrastination, perfectionism, anxiety, or even burnout. You may not consciously think, 'I'm afraid to be successful,' but your body hesitates, your mind stalls, and your calendar mysteriously fills up with distractions.

Sometimes your hidden driver is hiding in plain sight, disguised as a strength. Being endlessly accommodating may actually be a way of avoiding rejection. Perfectionism may be a mask for the fear of being judged. Even ambition, when rooted in the need to prove worth, can become a hidden driver in itself—driving you to chase achievements not out of joy, but out of survival.

We also have to address the role of emotional memory in how these drivers are encoded. *The brain remembers pain—emotional, social, or physical—far more intensely than neutral or even pleasurable experiences.* That means a single moment of humiliation in third grade, a parent's disapproval, or a teacher's dismissal can imprint a powerful message: 'Don't ever do that again.' *That becomes a driver. A quiet, constant steering mechanism toward safety rather than expansion.*

One client described it like this: 'It's like I've got a scared version of me whispering warnings I didn't even know I still believed.' When we began unpacking that whisper, we discovered that her fear of public speaking had nothing to do with a lack of skill. *It traced back to a moment in childhood when she was laughed at for sharing her ideas too enthusiastically. That moment created a hidden rule: 'Hide your passion. It's embarrassing.'*

That rule—unseen, unchallenged—ran her life for two decades. Until she met it with compassion, questioned its truth, and wrote a new internal rule: 'My passion inspires others. It's safe to speak up.'

Here's a powerful journaling practice to try: Complete the sentence, 'I'm afraid if I fully go after this goal, then _____.' Keep going. Let the sentence finish itself multiple ways. Don't edit. Just listen. *The answers may seem irrational, dramatic, or even silly. But they are gold. They're the voice of your hidden driver. And you can't work with what you can't hear.*

You can also tune into your physical responses. Your body is a powerful ally in this work. *Does your chest tighten when you imagine success? Do your shoulders rise when you visualize visibility? Do you feel a sense of guilt when you imagine earning more than your parents ever did? These are clues—not to be judged, but to be explored.*

Here's another exercise: Imagine your desired goal is fully achieved. You have the money, the love, the influence, the freedom. Now, ask yourself: What would I lose? What would I have to give up? Who might not approve? These aren't questions to derail your ambition—they're tools to surface the unspoken narratives your subconscious is holding onto.

Sometimes the hidden driver is legacy. You might be carrying beliefs passed down from generations. 'People like us don't get rich.' 'Stay humble or life will humble you.' 'Success comes with sacrifice.' **These inherited narratives become internalized truths that shape your self-concept and filter your behavior—even if you don't believe them consciously.**

To shift this, you must consciously reclaim authorship over your story. You must **question the sources of your beliefs and ask: Are these truths... or traditions?** Are these values... or vows I never agreed to? This is how you shift from inherited limitation to intentional creation.

Let's not underestimate how courageous this work is. Facing your hidden driver is not for the faint of heart. It requires honesty, self-compassion, and the willingness to go beyond your well-rehearsed surface answers. But the reward? Freedom. Authenticity. Movement where there was once stagnation.

One more client story. Janice had tried for years to scale her consulting business. Every time she gained momentum, she pulled back. She thought it was burnout or bad timing. When we explored deeper, it turned out she carried an unconscious loyalty to her father, who had worked in a blue-collar job all his life. Janice feared that succeeding too far would mean betraying her family's identity and losing the connection she had with them. Her hidden driver was loyalty, and staying connected to the people she loved and needed in her life—noble, but misapplied.

Once Janice acknowledged this, she was able to reframe: 'I honor where I come from—and I expand beyond it. My success is not a betrayal and I will not lose them, it's a continuation of my family's evolution.' With this new driver, she scaled her business within months—and felt emotionally free doing it.

This chapter isn't about blaming your past. It's about giving yourself new choices. The hidden driver was created to protect. But you're no longer a child who needs to hide or be protected. You are an adult who can choose a new path—with clarity, courage, and conscious alignment.

So, take time. Listen deeply. The hidden driver may be the part of you that's been waiting the longest to be heard.

In Chapter Eight, we'll explore why willpower—on its own—so often fails in the presence of these subconscious patterns, and what actually 'does' work to shift behavior and unlock lasting success.

CHAPTER 8

WHY WILLPOWER FAILS

Willpower is often hailed as the hero of success. From motivational talks to best-selling books, it's glorified as the core driver behind achievement. You just need more discipline, more grit, more motivation and determination. Right? But if you've ever set a goal and watched yourself fall back into old habits despite the best intentions, you already know willpower alone doesn't work.

It's not because you're lazy. It's not because you're weak. It's because willpower was never designed to carry the weight we put on it.

Think of willpower like the gas pedal in a car. It helps you move forward. But if the wheels are misaligned or the engine is faulty, pressing the pedal harder just burns more fuel without making meaningful progress. *In the same way, applying more pressure through willpower doesn't resolve internal misalignment—it only exhausts you.*

In fact, **studies in neuroscience have shown that willpower is a limited resource. Like a battery, it drains over time.** Stress, fatigue, decision-making, and emotional turmoil all deplete your reserves. And once your willpower battery runs low, old patterns automatically kick back in—because they're familiar, easy, and embedded in your subconscious.

Here's the kicker: **about 95% of our behavior is run by the subconscious mind. That means only 5% of your daily decisions are actually governed by conscious thought and willpower.** So, what happens when your 5% conscious goal runs up against a 95% subconscious habit, fear, or belief? You guessed it—the 95% wins.

This explains why so many resolutions fizzle. Why we repeat the same emotional patterns in relationships. Why we start and stop diets, projects, or routines. It's not because we don't want change—**it's because a deeper part of us is resisting it.** And that part can't be forced into submission by sheer will. It has to be understood.

Let's use another metaphor: **imagine trying to drive cross-country with the parking brake on. You can push forward, you can burn fuel, and you might even move a little—but eventually, the system overheats. That's what willpower-based change looks like.** Effort without ease. Movement without sustainability.

So, what's really going on when willpower fails? It's a sign that your internal systems are in conflict. **Your conscious mind says 'go,' while your subconscious mind says 'no.'** And if those two parts aren't on the same team, the subconscious will always win—because **it controls your emotions, your habits, your impulses, and even your self-image.**

Let's say you want to build a business, but deep down you carry a belief that success makes people selfish. Or that wealthy people lose their relationships. Or that if you shine too brightly, you'll be criticized or rejected. **These subconscious beliefs act like invisible anchors.** You might sprint ahead for a while, but eventually you'll hit a wall—one you can't see but can absolutely feel.

This is where most people blame themselves. They think they need more motivation, more self-control, or a better planner. **But what they actually need is alignment.** They need every part of them—the conscious and subconscious, the logical and emotional—pulling in the same direction.

Alignment doesn't mean perfection. It means inner agreement. It means no longer dragging parts of yourself that don't believe in the goal. Instead, you bring those parts into the conversation, understand their concerns, and create a new internal contract where success doesn't mean danger, loss, or disconnection.

One of the most overlooked reasons willpower fails is because we've been taught to override rather than relate. To fight against fear instead of listening to it. To silence doubt instead of decoding it. But the subconscious doesn't need suppression. **It needs negotiation. It needs to feel safe before it lets go of the old and embraces the new.**

When clients come to me stuck in cycles of self-sabotage, *I always ask: What might be the hidden benefit of staying stuck?* What fear could be connected to moving forward? These aren't easy questions, but **they unlock the real reason willpower isn't working.** And once you discover that, the change becomes not only possible—but inevitable.

Take a moment to think of a goal you've struggled to achieve. Now ask yourself: What part of me might be scared to reach it? What would change if I got it? Who might not approve? What might I lose? **These are doorways to understanding—and ultimately dissolving—the resistance beneath the surface.**

When alignment happens, things feel different. You no longer need to push. You're pulled. You're not climbing uphill with a backpack full of conflicting beliefs. You're walking a clear path. And that's when your energy returns. Your focus sharpens. Your progress accelerates—without the burnout.

So, if willpower hasn't worked for you, good. It means you're ready for a deeper way. A better way. A way that honors the full truth of who you are and how you're built.

In the next chapter, we'll explore how to uncover and transform the root beliefs that keep you stuck, and how to install new ones that make your goals inevitable—not because you pushed harder, but because you became aligned from the inside out.

CHAPTER 9

UNCOVERING CORE MISBELIEFS

Most people never stop to ask where their beliefs come from. They simply operate through them—making choices, forming opinions, reacting to life—all while assuming their lens is reality. But **our beliefs are not facts. They're interpretations. Stories. Conclusions we drew in moments of confusion, fear, or longing.** And many of them are outdated or simply untrue.

These are what we call **core misbeliefs: unconscious ideas about ourselves, others, and the world that shape our identity and behavior without our full awareness.** They tend to form early, stick hard, and rarely get questioned. You didn't choose them—they were absorbed, inherited, or emotionally imprinted. **But until you challenge them, they run the show.**

Core misbeliefs sound like: 'I'm not good enough.' 'If I'm successful, people will leave me.' 'Love has to be earned.' 'I don't deserve happiness.' 'Something always goes wrong.' The tragedy is that these beliefs become self-fulfilling. *When you believe success equals danger, your brain filters out opportunities or causes you to self-sabotage. When you believe love must be earned, you over give and exhaust yourself, attracting takers instead of partners.*

And the worst part? **These beliefs usually come from our most vulnerable moments—childhood misunderstandings, emotional pain, rejection, or shame.** Maybe your parents scolded you when you expressed joy. Maybe your teacher humiliated you in front of the class. Maybe a sibling overshadowed you. You decided, consciously or not: 'It's safer to hide. It's dangerous to be seen.' And from that moment on, hiding became your strategy for survival.

Now, as an adult, you may consciously want to shine, to lead, to love, to succeed—but your inner system is still following that old survival rule. **This is where the misbelief becomes the silent saboteur.**

Identifying these beliefs requires honesty and gentleness. You're not trying to expose a flaw—you're uncovering a defense. A protective logic formed by a younger version of you who did their best with limited tools.

Here's one method to reveal them: Look at a recurring life struggle. Maybe it's financial. Maybe it's about relationships. Maybe it's visibility or trust. Then ask**: 'What would someone have to believe in order to keep recreating this pattern?' Write your answers without editing. Let your subconscious speak.**

Another method: Pay attention to your emotional spikes—moments where you feel shame, rage, anxiety, or panic. **What just happened? What did you tell yourself in that moment?** Those thoughts are breadcrumbs leading to a belief.

You can also complete these prompts: 'I always...' 'People never...' 'I'm afraid that...' or 'If I succeed...' These sentence starters are powerful because they bypass the rational mind and tap directly into the narratives you've internalized.

Remember: misbeliefs don't have to be logical. In fact, they rarely are. **The belief 'If I shine, I'll be punished' may sound absurd—until you remember how you were teased for excelling. The belief 'If I have more, others will have less' may feel noble—until you realize it's keeping you broke.**

Once you've identified a core misbelief, don't rush to replace it. First, thank it. It served a purpose. It tried to protect you. Then gently question it. Ask: 'Is this always true?' 'Where did I learn this?' 'What else could be true?'

From there, you begin the realignment process: writing new beliefs that serve your current vision, not your past fears. Beliefs like: 'It's safe to be seen.' 'My success uplifts others.' 'I'm allowed to receive without guilt.' 'I'm lovable, even when I'm not performing.'

These new beliefs must be repeated, embodied, and felt. Your subconscious won't believe them at first. That's okay. You're planting seeds. **Over time, with consistency and compassion, they begin to take root.** And as they do, your actions, habits, and results begin to shift automatically.

This is not a quick fix. But it is a lasting one. Because once you change your core misbeliefs, you don't have to fight yourself anymore. You're no longer living someone else's script. **You're writing your own story—from clarity, from truth, and from power.**

Let's take a deeper look at how these misbeliefs shape entire trajectories of our lives. Imagine a child who learns that their worth is conditional on achievements—only praised when bringing home perfect grades or awards. This child may grow into an adult who chases success relentlessly, not from inspiration, but from fear. Every accomplishment becomes a way to earn love, not a celebration of their own growth. Their belief? 'I am only valuable if I achieve.' This misbelief creates burnout, imposter syndrome, and an endless loop of striving without fulfillment.

Others may carry beliefs rooted in abandonment. A parent's unpredictable affection, or a caregiver's emotional unavailability, can plant the seed of 'I am too much' or 'I'm a burden.' These beliefs often manifest as chronic people-pleasing, avoidance of intimacy, or over-apologizing for existing. Until these beliefs are addressed and gently rewritten, they silently dictate relationship patterns, career choices, and even self-worth.

Another layer to this work involves recognizing that we often reinforce our own misbeliefs through confirmation bias. If you believe that people can't be trusted, you'll unconsciously seek out situations that validate that idea. *If you believe you don't belong, you'll notice every exclusion and overlook every invitation. The brain is wired to protect your identity—even if that identity is rooted in pain.* Changing a misbelief means changing your self-concept, which requires conscious effort and emotional courage.

Sometimes the origin of a misbelief isn't even your own experience. It's generational. Passed down like a family heirloom. Maybe you grew up hearing stories of financial struggle, watching your parents fear success, or absorbing cultural narratives about limitation. These beliefs are no less powerful for being inherited—*they live in the nervous system, in your language, in your body. But the good news? You can be the one to break the chain.*

One transformative tool is to externalize the belief. *Write it on paper. Speak it out loud. Create a dialogue. Ask it questions. Where did you come from? What were you trying to protect me from? What do you need in order to let go?* This approach transforms the belief from a silent saboteur to a visible, addressable thought form. You begin to see that it isn't you—it's something you once learned, and *what is learned can be unlearned.*

It's important to remember that misbeliefs aren't removed in one dramatic epiphany. Often, they dissolve gradually. A conversation here. A new experience there. Bit by bit, the emotional charge softens. You find yourself reacting differently. Making braver choices. Feeling more at peace in your own skin. That's the real sign of transformation—not perfection, but freedom.

So be patient with this process. Be kind to yourself. The beliefs that held you back were once the beliefs that held you together. But you're not that child anymore. *You're the one holding the pen now, writing a new story—and that story begins with truth.*

CHAPTER 10

THE ALIGNMENT METHOD – STEP BY STEP

By now, you've discovered that willpower isn't the path, and positive thinking isn't enough. You've explored the tug-of-war between conflicting goals and the hidden misbeliefs that silently steer your choices. So, what's the solution? It's alignment. And in this chapter, we'll walk step by step through a powerful process to achieve it.

Alignment means bringing your conscious and subconscious minds into agreement so that they're no longer pulling in opposite directions. It's about transforming resistance, not overpowering it. When you're aligned, you don't have to force action—you're naturally drawn forward by internal harmony.

The Alignment Method is built on five core phases: **Awareness, Investigation, Reconciliation, Realignment, and Integration.** Let's explore each.

1. **Awareness** – The first step is recognizing where the conflict lives. What goal have you been trying to achieve that keeps slipping through your fingers? Write it down clearly. Now ask yourself: What part of me doesn't want this? Be honest. No judgment. Awareness opens the door to transformation.

2. **Investigation** – Now that you've spotted the conflict, go deeper. What belief or fear lives underneath the resistance? Use tools from the last chapter—complete sentence stems like 'If I succeed...' or 'I'm afraid that...' Let the answers come without censoring. This is where many discover the root misbelief driving their sabotage.

3. **Reconciliation** – Once the root belief is visible, don't attack it. Thank it. It once served to protect you. Now begin a dialogue: 'What were you trying to do for me?' 'What do you need to feel safe letting go?' Reconciliation acknowledges the part of you that held the old belief and honors it for its intent—even if its impact was limiting.

4. **Realignment** – This is where you craft a new belief, one that serves your present goals, not past fears. 'It's safe to succeed.' 'I can be visible and still be loved.' Make sure your new belief is not just affirming—it needs to feel believable. Start where you are. If 'I'm wildly successful' feels false, begin with 'I'm learning how to allow success.' Your new belief must feel emotionally true to start gaining traction.

5. **Integration** – Now you bring your new belief into daily life. Practice it mentally. Speak it aloud. Visualize living it. Catch the old narrative when it arises and gently reframe. Integration turns insight into identity. It's the repetition of your new aligned belief—especially in emotional moments—that rewires the brain and reconditions your habits.

Let's look at a simple real-world example. Suppose your conscious goal is to build a thriving business, but your subconscious holds the belief from your childhood that wealthy people are selfish or disconnected. You'll likely struggle to grow, undercharge, or self-sabotage when success starts to build. There's a deeply rooted fear that many people carry without realizing it — a fear that if they become too successful, too bold, too different, they will lose the acceptance of the very people they once depended on for survival. As children, we needed the people who gave us food, shelter, and a sense of belonging. Their approval meant safety. Their disapproval, on a primal level, felt like a threat to our very existence.

So if the version of you that you're striving to become — confident, successful, visible — clashes with the role your family once accepted or tolerated, a powerful inner conflict begins to form. Subconsciously, the mind says: *If I become that person, I might be rejected. I might be cut off. I might lose love, connection, and identity.*

And here's the key: if this internal conflict were conscious — if you *knew* this was what was happening — you could reason with it. You could untangle the fear, work through the emotional knots, and find a way forward that honored both your truth and your past.

But it rarely works that way.

Instead, the fear stays hidden — buried so deep it never reaches the light of your conscious awareness. And from the shadows, it silently guides your behavior. It pulls your strings, limits your reach, and moves you across the board of life like a chess piece — without your permission and without your full understanding.

Until it's exposed, it continues to win.

Using the Alignment Method, **you'd begin by acknowledging the sabotage—not with shame, but with curiosity.** You'd uncover the belief about wealth and see how it tried to protect you from becoming isolated or losing connection. **You'd then craft a new truth: 'I can be wealthy and deeply connected.'** You'd rehearse this belief, not just intellectually, but emotionally—until your nervous system sees it as safe and true.

What's crucial here is that alignment is not a one-time event. It's a living practice. As you grow, new misalignments may surface—and that's not failure. **It's refinement. Each time you realign, you step into a clearer, more powerful version of yourself.**

Sometimes people ask, 'But what if I don't feel the new belief yet?' That's okay. **Start by acting as if it's true. Let the behavior lead the belief. Say it until it feels more familiar than foreign. With repetition and emotional reinforcement, your subconscious will adapt.** The brain loves repetition. Use it to your advantage.

The Alignment Method restores your agency. Instead of being hijacked by fear, you become an ally to your own mind. Instead of running on old programming, you install new scripts that match your desires. And when your inner world agrees, your outer results begin to reflect that harmony.

This isn't about perfection. You'll still have days where old patterns whisper. But now, you'll know what to do. You won't spiral—you'll realign. You won't fight—you'll collaborate with your mind, turning resistance into momentum.

In the next chapter, we'll explore how to strengthen this new alignment by bringing thought and emotion into deeper coherence. Because when your beliefs and feelings line up, you move from effort into flow.

Here's something worth remembering: **the Alignment Method is not about fixing you—it's about freeing you. You are not broken. You are not behind. You're a complex, brilliant human being who developed survival strategies based on past needs.** What we're doing here is updating your internal software to reflect your current truth, not your childhood script.

Let's also talk about resistance. **Many people feel a kind of pushback when they start doing alignment work. That's completely normal.** You might notice tiredness, distraction, or even emotional fog. This is your subconscious testing the safety of change. Think of it like stretching a muscle that hasn't moved in years—*it's going to resist before it releases.*

To soften resistance, **bring in practices that activate safety in your body. Breathwork, grounding exercises, music that soothes or energizes you. The subconscious responds more to emotion than logic**—so give it experiences that prove: 'Change is safe. Growth is safe. I am safe.'

Another key aspect of alignment is language. How you speak to yourself creates internal momentum. **Start listening to your inner narration. Do you speak with pressure or encouragement? Do you say, 'I have to succeed,' or 'I get to grow'?** The way you talk to yourself frames your reality. Align your language, and your mindset begins to follow.

Also, don't underestimate the power of journaling in this process. Writing connects the conscious and subconscious minds in a profound way. Try this exercise: write a letter from your future self—three years from now—who is already living the success you desire. Ask them: What did I do differently? What did I stop believing? What surprised me along the way? This letter becomes a blueprint for who you're becoming.

Visualization can also deepen alignment. Close your eyes and imagine living your new belief. What do you see? How do you feel in your body? Who are you with? What's different in your day?

Vivid visualization isn't just mental rehearsal—it's neurobiological programming. The brain doesn't distinguish well between imagined and real experiences. Use that to your benefit.

Finally, surround yourself with alignment. Read books that reflect your new identity. Spend time with people who model the success you're cultivating. Even your physical environment matters. Is your space aligned with who you're becoming? Small shifts—like clearing clutter or adding inspiring visuals—can reinforce big internal changes.

This chapter may offer more tools than you'll use at once, and that's okay. Pick one or two that resonate most right now. Master those. Then return and layer in more as you grow. **Alignment is not a race—it's a rhythm.**

CHAPTER 11

REALIGNING THOUGHT AND EMOTION

Alignment isn't just a matter of what you think—it's also about what you feel. **True transformation happens when thought and emotion are moving in the same direction.** This is where most people stumble. They say affirmations, visualize success, or mentally set goals, but emotionally they feel doubt, fear, or unworthiness. **The result? The subconscious picks up the emotional signal, not the mental one.**

The subconscious mind communicates through emotion. It doesn't understand bullet points or spreadsheets—it understands patterns of feeling. If you say, 'I'm successful,' but your body tenses and your stomach knots, the message is distorted. **Your words are saying one thing, but your emotional state is saying another. The subconscious always believes the stronger signal—and that's usually emotion.**

That's why this chapter is devoted to bringing emotional alignment into the process. When your beliefs and emotions agree, your actions become fluid. You don't have to push yourself—you move forward with energy and confidence. **This is the sweet spot of flow, where manifestation feels like momentum rather than struggle.**

The first step is emotional awareness. Most people are emotionally under-literate—they feel 'bad' or 'good,' but they can't identify the texture of the emotion. Is it anxiety or anticipation? Guilt or grief? Disappointment or dread? **The more precisely you can name what you're feeling, the more power you have to shift it.** Labeling emotion engages the prefrontal cortex, which helps regulate the nervous system and create space for change.

Next is emotional acceptance. You can't align with what you're resisting. Trying to force positive emotions while ignoring fear only buries the conflict deeper. **Instead, acknowledge the feeling fully. Say, 'I'm afraid of failing. I feel ashamed. I feel left behind.' Speak it without judgment.** Emotions that are acknowledged begin to move. Emotions that are denied become embedded.

Now comes the emotional pivot. Ask: What would I like to feel instead? **Your goal isn't to flip a switch—it's to shift the dial.** Move from **fear to curiosity, from dread to openness, from self-doubt to self-inquiry.** These are small, manageable steps. Emotional alignment isn't about perfection—it's about movement.

A powerful way to bring thought and feeling together is through emotionally charged affirmations. Choose one belief you're working on—like, 'It's safe to be seen.' Then recall a time when you felt seen and supported. Close your eyes. Feel that moment. Let your body remember the sensation. Now speak the affirmation from that emotional place. This is how you build congruence between thought and feeling.

Breathwork can also bridge the gap. Conscious breathing calms the nervous system, increases oxygen flow, and creates emotional spaciousness. **When you feel overwhelmed, try box breathing: inhale for four counts, hold for four, exhale for four, hold for** *four. Repeat.* This simple practice grounds your body and clears emotional static so that new thoughts can land.

Visualization is another emotional alignment tool—when done properly. Don't just see the picture. **Feel the scene. Engage your senses. If you imagine a future where you're living your dream, ask:** What do I hear? What do I smell? What's the texture of the clothes I'm wearing? The more vivid the emotional imprint, the more your subconscious registers it as real.

Movement and embodiment are also critical. The body stores emotional memory. When you move intentionally—whether through dance, walking, stretching, or posture shifts—you create space for new emotions to flow. **Even something as simple as standing tall and breathing deeply can shift your state from anxiety to empowerment.** Let your body teach your mind what's possible.

One more powerful exercise: practice emotional rehearsals. **Before a big meeting, a conversation, or a goal-setting session, take a few minutes to tune in emotionally. Ask: How do I want to feel during and after this? Then rehearse that emotion. Feel it in advance.** When the moment arrives, your nervous system already knows what to do.

As you develop emotional alignment, you'll notice new ease in your actions. You'll no longer feel like you're dragging yourself toward success. **You'll feel pulled, invited, supported—from within.** This is the power of coherence. It's the difference between rowing against the current and being carried by the tide.

Thoughts set direction, but emotions provide propulsion. When both are aligned, you move swiftly and surely toward what you desire. But more importantly, you feel good along the way. **And**

feeling good is not just a byproduct of success—it's the signal that you're aligned with it.

You are not meant to force your way into the life you want. You are meant to align with it, emotionally and mentally, so that it flows toward you with grace.

Let's pause to reflect on why this work is so important. If your mind believes one thing and your body feels another, you're constantly sending mixed signals—**not just to the world, but to yourself.** This internal noise creates energetic interference. You might look confident but inside feel unworthy. You might say you're ready but emotionally brace for disappointment. Your results, inevitably, reflect the confusion.

This is why **realigning thought and emotion is foundational**—it brings you into coherence. Think of coherence like tuning an instrument. **A guitar string that's even slightly off can throw off the entire song. But when tuned with precision, every note resonates beautifully.** The same is true of you.

One surprising insight that helps emotional realignment is realizing that most emotions are not problems—they're messengers. Fear may be saying, 'Slow down and consider your next step.' Sadness may be saying, 'Let go of what no longer fits.' Even anger, when explored constructively, can illuminate a boundary you've ignored. **Instead of reacting to emotions, ask what they're trying to tell you. This shifts you from resistance to relationship—with yourself.**

It's also valuable to learn how emotional patterns become somatic habits. If you've spent years suppressing sadness or over-activating cheerfulness to avoid rejection, **your body adapts to those roles.**

You carry that adaptation into every room you enter, often unconsciously. But once you notice the pattern, you can soften it. You can exhale the mask. You can let your body practice new emotional expressions—ones that match who you are now, not who you had to be.

Creating **alignment also requires compassionate patience**. Emotional rewiring isn't instant. **Some beliefs are entangled with trauma, attachment, or identity. Give yourself room. Celebrate incremental progress**. If you move from self-judgment to self-neutrality, that's success. If you go from dread to dull discomfort, that's movement. **Be as kind to your internal evolution as you would be to a friend learning to walk again**.

Support your alignment journey by **building rituals around emotional congruence. Light a candle while setting your intention for the day. Keep a morning journal that asks not just what you're doing—but how you want to feel. Listen to music that evokes your desired emotion** before a challenging task. Stack your environment in ways that anchor your chosen inner state.

You can also leverage mirror work. Speak your new belief aloud while looking into your own eyes. It might feel awkward at first— **but you're creating neural familiarity. You're allowing your face, tone, and presence to become allies, not critics**. This intimacy with self is what anchors emotional truth.

In a world full of external noise and mental strategies, emotional alignment becomes a quiet superpower. It gives you presence. It makes your intentions believable—not just to others, but to your subconscious. **And when belief and feeling merge, that's when everything changes.**

Let this chapter be your reminder: **you are not just a mind trying to think better thoughts. You are a whole system.** Thought and emotion. Mind and body. And the more you integrate them, the more unstoppable—and fulfilled—you become.

Let's take this a step further with a deeper exploration of what emotional dissonance feels like in everyday life. **Imagine setting a goal to start your own business. You're excited, energized, and your mind races with ideas. But the moment you sit down to make a plan, your stomach knots up. You start procrastinating. You find reasons to clean the house or check your email instead.** What's happening here isn't laziness—*it's emotional misalignment.* Your conscious desire is moving forward, but your emotional memory is pulling the brakes.

This inner tug-of-war is often driven by past emotional associations. Maybe the last time you took a big risk; you were judged or rejected. Maybe you failed and felt embarrassed. Your subconscious stores these experiences as cautionary tales. **So even though your mind wants to pursue success, your body remembers the cost. To move forward, you have to work with both—not override one with the other.**

That alignment doesn't mean constant joy or enthusiasm. Emotional alignment means you are honest about how you feel and willing to meet that feeling with compassion and curiosity. If you feel scared, you don't need to suppress it—you need to walk with it. **Ask it what it wants to show you. Emotions become allies when we stop treating them as enemies.**

Another **powerful tool** in emotional realignment is **emotional reframing.** Reframing isn't about denying a negative experience—it's about finding a new lens to view it through. For instance, instead of thinking 'I failed at my last relationship,' you might reframe it as **'I learned deeply about my needs and boundaries, and I'm more prepared now than ever.'** This changes the emotional association from shame to empowerment.

Let's also consider the role of emotional triggers. When we're emotionally triggered, we often revert to old patterns of protection— **shutting down, lashing out, avoiding.** These are learned defense mechanisms, not character flaws. Identifying your triggers is the first step. Then you can gently begin to deconstruct the emotional charge. **Ask: What old story is this reminding me of? Is it true now, or just familiar?**

Sometimes, **aligning thought and emotion requires help from outside ourselves.** This might mean therapy, coaching, or healing work that allows you to revisit old wounds with support. **Emotional alignment is not always a DIY project. It's courageous to ask for help—and wise to recognize when you need it.**

As your **emotional fluency increases, you'll begin to notice subtle shifts. Decisions feel clearer. Conflict becomes less reactive. Your desires no longer feel like distant hopes**—they feel like natural outcomes of who you are becoming. And perhaps most powerfully, you'll feel more at peace with yourself. That is the truest form of alignment.

Let's close this chapter with a practice. Each night before bed, reflect on this question: 'Where was I emotionally aligned today?' Celebrate that moment. Then ask: 'Where was I out of alignment?' Without judgment, trace the moment back. What were you thinking? What were you feeling? What might that feeling have been trying to protect? **Just becoming aware of this begins to dissolve the pattern.**

With time, **emotional alignment becomes your default mode.** You don't have to fight yourself to move forward—you simply flow in the direction you've chosen. **It won't always be easy. But it will be clear. And clarity, combined with self-compassion, is one of the most powerful states you can live from.**

CHAPTER 12

REWRITING THE INTERNAL CONTRACT

Every belief we carry—especially the ones we don't question—acts like a contract we signed with ourselves long ago. **These internal contracts form the terms of how we experience life. They dictate how much success we'll allow, how much love we'll accept, and how much happiness we'll trust.** Most of them were formed before we even knew we were signing anything.

Some of these contracts served us well at one time. They protected us from pain or rejection. They helped us make sense of chaos. But eventually, these old agreements outlive their usefulness. They begin to restrict rather than protect. What once was safety becomes a cage.

Rewriting the internal contract means identifying and updating the outdated rules you've been living by. **These rules are often phrased as absolutes: 'I must always be perfect.' 'I can't trust anyone.' 'Success means I'll be alone.' Each of these is a contract clause—and each one can be rewritten.**

The first step is to recognize the signature on the contract. Whose voice wrote this belief? Was it a parent's fear? A teacher's criticism? A culture's expectation? Often, these beliefs are inherited, not chosen. **Once we realize they were never really ours, we begin to regain the power to change them.**

Let's break down a contract. Suppose your old belief is: 'If I speak up, I'll be rejected.' This belief likely formed during a moment of vulnerability. You expressed something important and were met with dismissal or punishment. **The subconscious took a snapshot and created a clause: Stay silent to stay safe.**

To rewrite it, you begin by acknowledging the old contract's intention—protection. **Then you challenge its validity.** Is it always true? Is it still true? You create a new clause: **'When I speak with honesty, I connect more deeply.'** You then reinforce this clause with new experiences, gradually building trust in the new agreement.

It helps to write these new contracts out—literally. Create a document. Title it: 'My New Contract With Myself.' Write your revised beliefs. Sign it. Date it. **This symbolic act signals to your subconscious that a shift has occurred.**

Like any contract, the new one needs to be referenced often—especially at first. You may fall back into old terms when stressed or triggered. That's not failure. It's just the old programming showing itself. Gently return to the new agreement. Read it aloud. Feel it in your body. Visualize acting from it.

Remember: rewriting internal contracts is not about pretending the past didn't happen. It's about updating your operating system to match who you are now—not who you had to be then.

Let's explore how these internal contracts show up in everyday life. Maybe you have a deep desire to grow your company—but every time success increases to build, you pull back. You procrastinate. You self-sabotage. **Why? Because beneath the surface is an old** agreement that says: *'If I become too successful, people won't like me.' Or 'Success will separate me from my family.'* The old contract wasn't made consciously—**but it's still being enforced subconsciously.**

These kinds of patterns are frustrating because they create a gap between what you consciously want and what you subconsciously allow. You may feel like you're driving with one foot on the gas and the other on the brake. Rewriting your internal contract is what finally removes that brake. It's the difference between trying to make success happen and allowing it to unfold with less resistance.

To identify your current contracts, look at any area of your life where progress feels consistently difficult—your finances, your relationships, your health. Ask yourself: 'What would I have to believe to keep experiencing this?' **Let your subconscious answer without censorship.** Often the hidden belief is **subtle but powerful**, like 'I don't deserve ease,' or 'If I shine, others will suffer.'

Journaling is a powerful method for bringing these contracts into the light. Start a page with: **'The rule I've been living by is...' Then write whatever comes to mind. Don't overthink it. Follow up with: 'This rule was created to protect me from...' Then finally: 'The new rule I choose is...' This simple process moves you from unconscious agreement to conscious authorship.**

Rewriting a contract isn't just about changing words—**it's about feeling your way into a new emotional reality.** If your old contract was, 'I have to earn love by being useful,' your new contract might be, 'I am lovable because I exist.' That's not just a sentence—it's an energetic shift. To make it stick, you'll need to practice embodying it.

This is where inner child work can be a useful companion. The version of you who made that original contract was likely very young. You were doing your best to feel safe, accepted, and secure. As the adult, you can now revisit that moment—not to relive the pain, but to offer comfort. You might imagine **holding your younger self and saying: 'You did the best you could. But we don't need that rule anymore. We're safe now. We're allowed to choose a different way.'**

It's also helpful to note how your nervous system responds to rewriting old rules. Change—even positive change—can trigger anxiety. That's not a sign you're doing it wrong; it's a sign you're shifting a long-held survival strategy. **Meet the discomfort with breath, movement, or grounding exercises. Let your body know: growth is not a threat.**

One of the most empowering practices you can engage in is writing a new declaration. This is a living document that affirms your new way of being. You might start it like this*:* **'I now choose to live by a new agreement. One that honors my value, supports my vision, and releases old roles that no longer serve me.'** Read this out loud each morning. Let it sink in. Let it become your new truth.

Remember, you're **not just breaking old contracts—you're making better ones.** Contracts that are rooted in worthiness, clarity, and freedom. Contracts that reflect your evolution rather than your survival.

Lastly, be patient with yourself. **Old agreements can be deeply wired**. They may reappear in stressful moments. **But with time, repetition, and compassion, the new agreements take hold**. And once they do, **they become the new normal**—the standard by which your life organizes itself.

This chapter is your invitation to stop living by default and start living by design. No more invisible rules dictating your limits. You get to decide. You get to renegotiate. And your life will shift as a result.

To deepen this transformation, it's **important to create new behavioral anchors that support the rewritten contracts.** If your new agreement is 'I am worthy of being seen and heard,' **look for small, consistent ways to live that truth. Speak up in a meeting**. Share a personal win with a friend. Wear something bold that expresses your confidence. These are not grand gestures—**they're daily reinforcements**. Action makes belief tangible.

Accountability can also enhance the integration process. **When appropriate, share your new agreement with someone you trust. Let them know what you're working on. Ask them to reflect back when they see you honoring it—or when they notice you slipping into the old terms.** Having someone mirror your growth helps it solidify faster.

You can also support this integration by tracking progress through what we might call an 'alignment journal.' **At the end of each day, jot down a moment when you noticed the old contract trying to reassert itself—and how you responded. Then write down one way you honored the new agreement.** Over time, these reflections reveal patterns, build confidence, and create forward motion.

One challenge many people face when rewriting internal contracts is grief. **Yes, grief. Because even dysfunctional agreements often carry an emotional attachment. Maybe the old contract helped you stay connected to a parent. Or made you feel needed. Or gave you a sense of identity.** Letting go of it might stir up sadness or disorientation. That's okay. Allow space for that emotion. You're not just changing a belief—you're closing a chapter.

Some people also feel guilt when releasing old contracts, especially if they involve setting boundaries or prioritizing themselves. **Remember: a contract that harms your well-being is not noble—it's outdated.** You can honor your past while still choosing a new future. This is your life, and you deserve for it to be aligned with who you truly are now.

Metaphorically speaking, rewriting your internal contract is like renovating a house you've lived in for decades. **You keep what's beautiful and strong, you remove what no longer fits, and you design for where you're going—not where you've been.** It takes effort, yes—but the reward is living in a space that finally feels like home.

One final exercise to seal this transformation: write a letter from your future self to your present self. This version of you has fully integrated the new agreement. What do they want you to know? What has changed in their life? What are they most proud of? **Let this letter be a love note from who you're becoming—to who you are now.**

Your inner world is always negotiable. You don't have to stay loyal to limitations. You're allowed to renegotiate your role, your rules, and your reality. That's not selfish. That's sovereignty. And it's the foundation for lasting success from the inside out.

CHAPTER 13

BUILDING SUCCESS FROM THE INSIDE OUT

Most people approach success from the outside in. They set goals. They chase achievements. They build systems and stack habits. And while these strategies can produce results, **they often leave something essential out of the equation: the self doing the work. True, lasting success—the kind that feels both fulfilling and sustainable—has to be built from the inside out.**

What does that mean? It means your inner world becomes the blueprint for your outer experience. **Your beliefs, your emotional patterns, your sense of worth—these are not invisible forces. They're architects.** They shape the choices you make, the risks you take, the relationships you nurture, and the results you create.

When you align your internal state with the outcomes you desire, success stops being a battle. It becomes a reflection. Instead of pushing, you're pulled. **Instead of chasing, you're attracting.** This is the difference between achievement that drains you and success that expands you.

One of the first steps to building from the inside out is shifting from outcome obsession to identity alignment. Most people ask, 'What do I want to have?' A more powerful question is, 'Who do I want to be?' **Because when you become the kind of person who naturally creates what you want, the outcome takes care of itself.**

This shift in identity requires more than visualization or positive thinking. **It requires congruence—your thoughts, feelings, and actions all aligned toward the same end.** If you want to be a confident leader, but your inner dialogue is filled with self-doubt, your actions will always carry hesitation. If you want to build wealth, but subconsciously believe money is dangerous, you'll find ways to repel it.

Building success from the inside out also means re-evaluating what success actually means to you. So much of what we strive for is inherited or projected: someone else's definition, someone else's dream. Pause and ask yourself: 'What does success look like on my terms? How does it feel? Who am I with? What impact am I making?' Let this vision be your guide—not external benchmarks.

One powerful practice is **future-casting. Imagine yourself one year from now, living your definition of success.** Walk through a day in that life. Where do you wake up? What's your energy like? What are you proud of? Let your senses get involved. This isn't fantasy—it's a rehearsal. You're wiring your system to become familiar with what's coming.

Success from the inside out is not about avoiding effort. **It's about directing your energy efficiently.** It means doing less of what depletes and more of what aligns. It means noticing when your motivation is fear-driven and gently reorienting to love, truth, and purpose. It means acting not from desperation, but from wholeness.

In the next section, we'll go deeper into the rituals, reflections, and real-world strategies that bring this inner alignment to life—so you're not just dreaming big but living aligned.

To truly build success from the inside out, you must learn how to listen to yourself in a deeper, more deliberate way. We've been trained to look outside for validation—checking the likes, the metrics, the feedback. But the most important signal is internal. How does this path feel in your body? Does your work energize you or exhaust you? Do you feel expansive or contracted when you think about your goals? These inner cues are data. Learning to trust them is a form of mastery.

Self-trust is a cornerstone of sustainable success. When you trust yourself, you're no longer at the mercy of trends or opinions. You can hear advice without being swayed. You can make bold moves without external permission. **Self-trust is not arrogance—it's inner clarity.** And clarity is magnetic.

Part of building success internally is also about integrating failure differently. Instead of seeing failure as a stop sign, you begin to view it as feedback. You understand that every misstep carries information. What didn't work? What was out of sync? What do you now know more clearly? **This growth mindset is what allows you to keep refining your path rather than abandoning it at the first sign of difficulty.**

Let's talk about emotional resilience, another vital piece of the puzzle. When your success is built on surface-level confidence, it's easily shaken. But when it's rooted in self-worth, it becomes durable. **Resilience doesn't mean never feeling doubt. It means you've learned to relate to doubt differently—you see it, acknowledge it, and move anyway. That's the emotional muscle that separates dreamers from doers.**

A highly effective practice in this journey is the inner alignment audit. On a regular basis—weekly or monthly—ask yourself three questions: **1) What feels aligned in my life and work right now?**

2) What feels out of alignment? 3) What would alignment look like in that area? Write your answers without filtering. The goal is to increase your awareness and take small steps toward greater internal cohesion.

One of the hidden benefits of inner alignment is peace. When you stop fighting yourself, you free up massive reserves of energy. You no longer waste effort second-guessing or trying to be someone you're not. Instead, you're able to channel your focus, creativity, and action in one unified direction. That's when results begin to feel not just possible—but inevitable.

This path also invites a shift in how we view ambition. In the traditional model, ambition is about climbing higher. In the inner-aligned model, ambition becomes about going deeper. It's not just **'What can I achieve?' but 'How can I become more of who I really am in the process?'** That kind of ambition creates a ripple effect—it influences others, uplifts systems, and inspires communities.

Let's not pretend this path is always easy. **It requires introspection, honesty, and the willingness to make tough choices. You may outgrow roles, relationships, or routines that once felt essential.** That's part of the deal. Inner growth creates outer change. **But what you gain is far more valuable: a life that reflects your values, a career that matches your calling, and success that feels like freedom—not pressure.**

Before we move on, try this integration exercise: **Write a letter from your future self—one year ahead, fully aligned, fully expressed.** Let them describe what their life looks like, how they feel, what they're proud of.

Let this letter serve as both inspiration and calibration. I**t's not a fantasy—it's a forecast of what's possible when you build from the inside out.**

CHAPTER 14

LIVING IN ALIGNMENT

Living in alignment is the culmination of all the inner work you've done up to this point. **It's not a destination you reach—it's a practice, a way of being, a state of inner congruence** that becomes the foundation for your outer world.

Alignment means your thoughts, feelings, values, and actions are moving in the same direction. **It means you're no longer torn between what you say you want and what you unconsciously resist.** It's not about being perfect. It's about being honest. Consistently. Courageously. And with increasing clarity.

In alignment, **you stop chasing what looks good and start living what feels true. You make decisions based on resonance, not fear.** You pursue goals because they nourish your soul, not just your resume. You say no to what drains you—even if it's familiar—and yes to what energizes you—even if it's new.

This alignment creates a kind of internal integrity that becomes magnetic. People sense it. Opportunities respond to it. You become more grounded, more focused, more impactful—not because you're trying harder, but because you're trying less to be someone else.

Living in alignment doesn't mean you won't face challenges. It means your response to them will be different. Instead of reacting from old patterns, you'll respond from presence. You'll recognize when something is off and adjust without shame. You'll trust yourself more. You'll need less approval from others. And that's freedom.

One of the most beautiful aspects of **alignment is that it simplifies your life**. You stop needing to control every outcome because you know you're showing up as your truest self. You stop overthinking every decision because you've created an internal compass. You become less busy and more effective. Less scattered and more fulfilled.

Let's be clear: ***alignment is not a luxury—it's a necessity for living a meaningful life. Without it, even your greatest achievements can feel hollow***. With it, even small moments become deeply satisfying. The peace you feel when your inner and outer lives match—***that's success.***

As you continue this journey, remember that alignment is a muscle you strengthen over time. ***You check in. You course correct. You stay curious. You stay honest.*** And when things fall out of sync, you don't collapse—***you realign.***

To live in alignment is to live in continual dialogue with yourself. It's not a one-time declaration—it's an ongoing practice of tuning in. You begin each day with presence. You end each day with reflection. And in between, you act in a way that honors your truth, even when it's inconvenient or uncomfortable.

The challenge with alignment is not knowing what's true—it's trusting what's true. So many of us have been taught to override our intuition in favor of logic, consensus, or tradition. But alignment doesn't live in the head alone. It lives in the body, the heart, the soul. **When something is right, you feel it. When something is off, you feel that too. The question is: are you willing to honor those feelings?**

Think of **alignment like a well-tuned instrument**. When each string is taut, calibrated, and responsive, beautiful music can emerge. **But when even one string is out of tune, everything feels dissonant.** Your values, your goals, your relationships, your energy—they all need to be attuned to the same frequency. That's what makes your life not just functional, but resonant.

Alignment is not about rigidity—it's about coherence. You're allowed to evolve. Your truth today might not be your truth next year. **Living in alignment doesn't require you to be static; it requires you to be honest about where you are, what matters now, and what you're called to next.**

One way to stay aligned is to create what I call a **personal alignment map**. It **includes your core values, your long-term vision, your emotional needs, your energetic boundaries, and your current goals. Revisit this map monthly.** Use it to guide decisions, assess opportunities, and evaluate your relationships. If something doesn't fit your map, it probably doesn't fit your life.

Another powerful practice is to **choose a word or phrase each week that represents the energy you want to embody. Maybe it's 'clarity,' or 'flow,' or 'courage.'** Write it on your mirror. Let it influence your tone, your pace, your posture. These small cues keep you rooted in intention, which is where alignment lives.

There's a kind of quiet confidence that develops when you live in alignment. You no longer feel the need to explain, defend, or justify your choices. You move with integrity. And that integrity becomes your reputation. People trust you—not because you're perfect, but because you're consistent. They know where you stand, because you know where you stand.

Living in alignment also means you stop abandoning yourself to keep the peace. You stop shrinking to be liked. You stop performing for approval. You realize that the cost of self-betrayal is too high, and the return on authenticity is great. You may disappoint others—but you will no longer disappoint yourself.

You'll notice that as your internal alignment grows, your outer world begins to reconfigure. You may attract different opportunities. You may lose certain connections—but gain more nourishing ones. You'll begin to feel a sense of grace moving through your life, not because it's easy, but because it's congruent. Things flow more naturally when you're not fighting your own current.

Alignment creates bandwidth. **When your inner and outer selves match, you have more energy. You're no longer leaking it through indecision, resentment, or pretense. That energy can now be invested in creation, connection, and contribution.**

Let's be real—living in alignment can be disruptive. It might call you to leave jobs, end patterns, walk away from dynamics that no longer support your growth. That's not failure. That's fidelity to your evolution. You are not here to remain unchanged. **You are here to expand into your truest expression. Alignment is how you get there.**

Here's a journaling prompt to work with: 'Where in my life am I saying yes when I mean no? And what would change if I honored my "no"?' Don't rush the answer. Let it surface slowly. Then write a companion prompt: 'Where am I holding back a yes that wants to be expressed?' **Alignment is often found in reclaiming both our sacred yes and our sacred no.**

And here's one final note: living in alignment doesn't make life perfect—it makes life real. There will still be hard days. There will still be doubts. But you'll meet those moments from a deeper place. A steadier place. A place that says, **'Even now, I trust myself.' That is what it means to live in alignment.**

CHAPTER 15

YOU HAD THE POWER ALL ALONG

By the time you reach this chapter, you've probably had moments of revelation. You've seen how your mind, your patterns, your beliefs—especially the hidden ones—have shaped the reality around you. You've uncovered internal conflicts, rewritten your own agreements, and taken steps toward a life built on alignment. Now, we return to a truth that has been quietly present through every page:

You had the power all along.

It's the kind of statement that seems obvious in hindsight, yet nearly impossible to believe in the beginning. **Because the journey to owning your power often starts with giving it away. To parents. To partners. To teachers. To employers. To systems. To self-doubt. At some point, you believed someone else knew better.** That someone else's permission or validation would make it real.

But true transformation happens the moment **you realize that no one is coming to rescue you—and no one needs to**. Because you were never broken. Just disconnected from the part of you that already knew what to do.

Owning your power doesn't mean never needing help. ***It means knowing the difference between support and surrendering your*** *authority. It means becoming the source of your own validation. It means listening to your truth, even when it's quiet.* Especially when it's quiet.

You had the power when you asked hard questions. You had the power when you chose to slow down instead of speeding up. You had the power when you walked away from things that no longer matched your values. **Power doesn't always roar. Sometimes it whispers. But it is always there—waiting for you to claim it.**

When you live from that space, you become less reactive and more responsive. You stop outsourcing your decisions. You trust your instincts. You welcome your emotions, not as obstacles, but as guides. **You allow discomfort to shape you, not define you. You live in partnership with life, not in resistance to it.**

Power, in this context, is not about dominance. It's about sovereignty. It's the quiet confidence of someone who knows their worth, who creates their path, and who respects others enough to not need control. This is what inner mastery looks like. **And it's available to anyone willing to remember their own strength.**

Let this final chapter serve not as a conclusion, but as a beginning. A beginning of deeper self-leadership, more radical authenticity, and a lifelong commitment to alignment. Your path is yours to walk—but you are never walking it alone.

You don't need a guru. You don't need another trend. What you need is already within you. And now, you have the tools to access it.

The shift you've been waiting for isn't outside of you. It's you.

There's something liberating about understanding that you don't have to wait anymore. For the right timing, the perfect circumstances, the green light from someone else. **You are the author now. That** *pen you once handed to others? You've reclaimed it. You're writing your own story—line by line—with intention.*

This empowerment isn't about grand gestures. In fact, it often shows up in the smallest ways. Saying no without guilt. Asking for what you want. Creating boundaries not as walls, but as invitations for healthier dynamics. Redirecting energy away from pleasing and toward creating. These are all forms of power. Quiet, consistent power.

Many people associate power with charisma, confidence, or control. But those are merely expressions. **Real power is presence. It's the ability to remain centered while the world around you sways.** It's the resilience to return to yourself when life tries to pull you off course. It's the choice to respond instead of react.

When you're in your power, you stop confusing performance for purpose. You no longer shape-shift to fit someone else's expectations. Instead, you bring your whole self to the table—flaws, gifts, opinions, intuition. You're not afraid to be misunderstood, because you're no longer trying to be universally approved. **You've stopped auditioning and started arriving.**

One of the most powerful transformations occurs when **you realize your past doesn't define your potential.** Whatever stories you've carried—of failure, of fear, of 'not enough'—can be rewritten. They don't disappear, but they no longer dictate. **You become the narrator, not the character trapped in a loop.**

You might be wondering, 'What if I forget this? What if I slip back into old habits?' That's okay. **Power doesn't require perfection. It thrives on practice.** You will forget. You will fall back. And you will rise again—faster, wiser, and more aware. Every stumble is an invitation to recommit to yourself.

The truth is, many people are more comfortable playing small than risking their power. **There's a false safety in staying invisible. But invisibility costs more than it protects. It robs the world of your presence. Your perspective. Your purpose. And most importantly, it robs 'you' of the experience of fully inhabiting your life.**

There's a reason so many transformational stories—from fairy tales to modern films—follow a similar arc: the protagonist forgets who they are, faces trials, and then reclaims their identity with new clarity. You're not reading this book by accident. **You're somewhere in that arc. You're remembering. You're reclaiming. And you're rewriting the ending.**

This power is not just for you. When you live from a place of alignment, you give others silent permission to do the same. **Your courage creates space. Your authenticity inspires possibility. You become a lighthouse—not by pushing, but simply by shining.**

It's easy to underestimate how powerful aligned, intentional living can be. The external world might not change overnight—but your experience of it will. **You'll begin to notice opportunities you once overlooked. You'll handle challenges with more ease. You'll feel safer in your own skin**. And most beautifully, you'll stop apologizing for existing.

Let's ground this with a real-life example. Imagine two professionals starting a new business. One is powered by misalignment—fear of failure, pressure to prove, constant comparison. The other is powered by alignment—a clear purpose, inner trust, grounded values. On paper, they may look the same. But over time, their energy, impact, and sustainability will reveal the difference. The aligned one will attract resonance, not just results.

Here's a simple yet profound practice to anchor your power each day: Start every morning with this statement—*'I choose to remember who I am.'* Then, before you go to bed, ask yourself—*'Did I honor who I am today?'* These bookend reflections keep you anchored in self-leadership.

The final message is this: **You don't have to earn your power. You only have to remember it. Reconnect with it. And take aligned action from it, even if it's small.** Especially when it's small. **These micro-movements become momentum. That momentum becomes identity. And that identity becomes your life.**

You've been on a journey throughout this book—**not just of learning, but of returning. Returning to the version of you that isn't fragmented by fear or bound by external scripts**. The version that stands steady in truth, walks freely in purpose, and creates from alignment.

This chapter is the reminder you'll want to revisit when you feel off-course. When the noise of life drowns out your inner voice. When the old doubts sneak back in. Come back to this: You had the power all along. You still do. And now, you know how to use it.

So much of personal growth has been framed around fixing ourselves, but what if the work is not about fixing—what if it's about finally listening? When you stop trying to force yourself into someone else's mold, your life begins to take on a shape that feels distinctly yours. That's not rebellion—it's remembrance.

Owning your power also means owning your pace. Some breakthroughs happen in a flash. Others unfold like a sunrise—quietly, steadily, undeniably. Don't compare your chapter to someone else's highlight reel. Your path has its own rhythm. Your power respects that rhythm. Let it guide you without shame.

If there's a hidden gift in the resistance you've faced, it's this: resistance has taught you how to be resilient. Every no you encountered externally gave you an opportunity to find a deeper yes within. Every setback refined your vision. Every detour taught you a new route. Power isn't about never falling—it's about always getting back up more aligned than before.

As you continue beyond this book, know that power will not always look like certainty. Sometimes, it looks like grace. Sometimes it looks like saying 'I don't know' with dignity. Sometimes it looks like choosing rest over proving or surrender over strategy. You're not abandoning ambition—you're aligning it.

The world needs people who remember their power—not to dominate, but to illuminate. You're now equipped to live as one of them. And in doing so, you'll help others remember theirs. In the next chapter you will be introduced to the hidden goal still running the show.

CHAPTER 16

HOW TO RECOGNIZE THE HIDDEN GOAL THAT'S STILL RUNNING THE SHOW

If you've ever found yourself wondering why things still feel just a little out of sync—even after doing so much of what you thought was right—this chapter will offer the clarity you've been looking for.

Because most people eventually sense it:

A subtle resistance.

A quiet tension beneath the surface.

That feeling that, despite your hard work and good intentions, something's not quite aligning.

You may be doing well. You may even be admired.

But deep down, something doesn't feel quite right.

You may sense:

- A nagging feeling that you're meant for more — but you're not sure how to reach it.

- A quiet disappointment that lingers, even when things seem "fine."
- A sense that you're holding back — but can't explain why.
- Subtle frustration when others praise your success, because it doesn't match how you feel inside.
- A heaviness around goals that once felt exciting.
- A recurring thought: *"Why does this still feel so hard?"*
- A sense of disconnection from the version of you that you know you could be.
- The feeling that you're playing a role — not fully living in your truth.
- A flicker of envy when you see someone else doing what you secretly wish you could.

These aren't failures.

They're signals.

Signs that a hidden story — a role you once had to play — may still be steering the outcome.

WHAT IS THE HIDDEN GOAL?

The hidden goal *isn't* your dream.

It's not the version of you who wants more success, better relationships, or a sense of inner freedom.

That's your **conscious** goal.

The hidden goal is different—and **far more powerful**.

It lives beneath your awareness, shaped by **emotional survival** long before you ever had language for it.

It's the role you adopted as a child to feel safe, accepted, and emotionally connected to the people around you.

Children will become whoever they need to be to feel that they belong—even if it means becoming someone they're not.

Because for a child, being ignored or emotionally exiled *is **unthinkable***.

So we adapt. We read the room. We figure out—quickly and quietly—who we need to be to get attention… or at least avoid rejection.

That role might have been:

- The quiet one
- The smart one
- The peacemaker
- The helper
- The scapegoat
- The not-as-good-as-your-sibling one
- The invisible one
- The one who always struggles
- The one who never outshines
- The perfect one

Whatever the role was, it gave you a place. A tether. A reason to be seen.

And once that identity is locked in, the subconscious mind holds onto it—**for *dear life.***

Because letting go of it could feel like letting go of your ability to exist.

This is where the fear of success comes in—not because you fear achievement itself, but because success would require you to step outside the role you were assigned. And that feels like emotional disconnection. A threat to belonging.

How This Creates Self-Sabotage

Fast forward to adulthood: You have goals. Big ones. You want to be successful. Free. Joyful. Empowered. Visible.

But now you're trying to build a **new life on top of an old identity.**

And that identity is still whispering:

"Don't go too far. Don't rise too high. **Don't be the person you weren't allowed to be."**

So your subconscious steps in with a solution:

Behaviors that look reasonable on the outside—but are secretly designed to hold you back.

Not to hurt you.

But to **protect you** from becoming **someone who doesn't "belong."**

And that's where the saboteurs come in.

WHAT THE SABOTEUR REALLY IS

The saboteur isn't a flaw. It's a shield.

It's the mechanism your subconscious uses to keep you in alignment with that old emotional contract.

Let's say your conscious goal is to be wildly successful—to shine, to lead, to break generational ceilings.

But as a child, you learned that being smart or independent made others uncomfortable. Maybe a parent discouraged your ideas, or a sibling was the "golden child," and you were always told not to compete. Maybe your success threatened someone, and you learned to dim your light to stay safe. Because we are all like snowflakes that are not the same we have our own patterns.

Now, as an adult, you start overthinking everything.

You plan, but don't act. You revise, but never release. You doubt yourself constantly.

On the surface, it looks like caution.

But it's actually your subconscious saying:

"Don't step into the role you were once punished for."

And so, you protect yourself—by holding back.

This is what the saboteur does. It's not "bad behavior."

It's a subconscious *strategy* to avoid emotional danger—even when that danger is long gone.

HOW TO USE THIS CHAPTER

In the next section, you'll meet some of the most common saboteurs I've seen in my decades of coaching and in my own life—behaviors that look like personality traits, but are really emotional armor.

You may see yourself in one. You may see yourself in several.

And that's okay—most people carry more than one survival role.

Each profile will show you:
- Name of the Saboteur

- How It Shows Up in Daily Life
- The Childhood Role It Grew From
- The Hidden Goal It's Trying to Fulfill
- What It's Costing You
- What to Start Noticing or Doing to Shift It

You do *not* need to fight your saboteur. You just need to understand it. Because once you can see what it's protecting—you can make a conscious choice to move beyond it.

And when you do? You'll stop circling your goals. You'll stop playing small. You'll stop second-guessing your instincts or waiting for someone else to give you permission.

Instead, you'll begin to feel something many people haven't felt in years—or maybe ever:

A sense of inner alignment.

Like your energy, your choices, and your direction finally match who you are on the inside.

You'll no longer be living through the lens of who others needed you to be.

You'll be living from a place that feels real, whole, and deeply yours.

Because that's what happens when the hidden goal is exposed:

You're no longer driven by invisible contracts from childhood.

You're no longer trying to earn your worth by staying small or acceptable.

You start choosing from truth—not fear.

And in that space, something opens.

The choices become clearer.

The pressure softens.

And the life you've been chasing—the one that always felt *just out of reach*—starts to feel not only possible... but natural.

You don't have to prove yourself anymore.

You just get to be yourself.

Fully. Authentically. Unapologetically.

Not who you were told to be.

Not who you had to be.

But who you actually are—and always were, beneath it all.

Recognizing the Saboteurs in Real Life

Now that you understand the hidden goal—the unconscious drive to stay connected by fulfilling a childhood role—let's look at how it *actually shows up* in daily life.

These profiles are not here to label you. They're here to help you *recognize the pattern*. To spot the unconscious roles you may still be performing, and gently bring them into awareness so you can finally shift them.

Let's begin with one of the most common and misunderstood saboteurs...

1. THE OVERTHINKER

How It Shows Up in Daily Life:

You analyze everything. You can't move forward without researching, weighing the pros and cons, playing out every possible scenario in your mind. You second-guess your instincts. You stall on decisions — not because you're unsure of your desires, but because you feel the need to "get it right" before taking the next step. Sometimes, the sheer volume of thinking becomes so overwhelming that you don't act at all.

The Childhood Role It Grew From:

Many Overthinkers were either discouraged from being confident — or punished, ignored, or dismissed when they did express clarity. Some were told directly or indirectly not to outshine a sibling or parent, or that they "always make bad decisions." Others were subtly conditioned to distrust their own knowing by caregivers who overrode their thoughts and feelings. To stay safe or accepted, they learned to hesitate... to defer... to question themselves before moving. Thinking became a buffer between their true self and external judgment.

The Hidden Goal It's Trying to Fulfill:

The Overthinker's hidden goal is to *not be seen as too capable, too decisive, or too bold.*

Why? Because those qualities may have once triggered emotional disconnection. Overthinking, then, becomes a way to **mute your potential** just enough to remain acceptable. It protects you from stepping into roles you weren't "allowed" to inhabit — like being the smart one, the leader, the one who actually knows what they want.

What It's Costing You:

Overthinking delays action. It waters down your power. It slowly erodes your confidence by creating constant doubt — and keeps you circling your dreams instead of stepping into them. People may see your intelligence but wonder why you never move. Opportunities pass. Time passes. And you remain stuck in thought while life keeps moving forward.

What to Start Noticing or Doing to Shift It:

- Start by asking yourself: "Who told me it wasn't safe to be decisive?" or "Whose approval did I lose when I acted on my instincts?"
- Watch for moments when you're "thinking in circles" and gently ask: "What am I afraid will happen if I trust myself here?"
- Begin taking small actions without having all the answers. Let yourself build proof that *clarity grows through movement*, not just reflection.
- Remind yourself: **You're not a child anymore. You don't have to dim your clarity to be loved or feel connected.**

Try This Exercise:

- List three important decisions you've delayed in the past six months.
- Write down what you were afraid would happen if you made the "wrong" choice.
- Now ask yourself: *Whose voice is that fear really coming from?*

- Finish by choosing one small action you can take toward resolution — even if it's imperfect. The goal is movement, not mastery.

-The truth is, your clarity was never the problem — only the fear of what it might cost you. But now that you see where the Overthinker was protecting you, you can begin to lead from trust instead of delay.

2. THE PROCRASTINATOR

How It Shows Up in Daily Life:

You delay. You put things off. You find a million small distractions before tackling the thing you know matters most. It's not that you're lazy — in fact, you may be busy all day — but you avoid the actions that move you toward your real goals. Deadlines sneak up. Dreams get postponed. You tell yourself you'll "start tomorrow"... and that tomorrow rarely comes.

The Childhood Role It Grew From:

For many procrastinators, productivity wasn't safe — it either brought unwanted attention or didn't bring the connection they were craving. Maybe you had a hyper-critical parent who never acknowledged your effort, no matter how hard you worked. Maybe success made others uncomfortable, or someone else in the family was "supposed" to be the achiever. Over time, it became safer to delay than to disappoint. You learned that doing nothing was less risky than doing something and feeling unseen, wrong, or disconnected.

The Hidden Goal It's Trying to Fulfill:

The procrastinator's hidden goal is to stay small enough to remain in alignment with the role you played in your family.

You learned that visible progress might bring criticism or emotional isolation. So by putting things off, your subconscious protects you from "stepping out of place." You delay—not because you don't want success, but because it doesn't feel emotionally safe to claim it.

What It's Costing You:

Procrastination keeps you in a cycle of frustration. You may feel ashamed, even confused — you know what to do, but you don't do it. It erodes self-trust and steals momentum. Over time, this pattern can lead to missed opportunities, financial strain, or simply a life that never quite feels like it got off the ground.

What to Start Noticing or Doing to Shift It:

- Ask yourself: "When I *don't* act, what uncomfortable outcome am I avoiding? Whose reaction am I protecting myself from?"
- Notice where you spend time on low-stakes tasks instead of what truly matters — and get curious, not judgmental.
- Experiment with micro-commitments: Set a timer for 10 minutes and do just *one thing* you've been avoiding. Prove to yourself that small steps are safe.
- Remind yourself: **Progress doesn't have to feel dangerous anymore. It's not disloyal to grow beyond what others expected of you.**

Try This Exercise:

- Write down three things you've been putting off, and next to each one, jot down what you fear will happen if you complete them.
- Then ask: *Whose expectations am I still afraid to violate?*
- Choose one task and take the smallest possible action — even if it's just opening a document, making a phone call, or writing a title.
- Notice how taking action shifts your energy — not because it's "done," but because you're no longer hiding from it.

-You weren't lazy — you were loyal. But now you get to be loyal to the future you, not just the version of you that once had to wait to feel safe.

3. THE PEOPLE-PLEASER

How It Shows Up in Daily Life:

You have a hard time saying no. You worry about disappointing others or being seen as selfish. You're quick to anticipate other people's needs and often put their comfort ahead of your own. Even when you're overwhelmed, you show up — with a smile. You may secretly resent how much you give, but you rarely voice it. You don't want to risk conflict, disapproval, or being seen as "too much."

The Childhood Role It Grew From:

People-pleasers often grew up in environments where love or attention felt conditional. You may have been praised when you were helpful, agreeable, or emotionally low-maintenance — and criticized or ignored when you weren't. If a parent was emotionally unavailable, angry, or unpredictable, you may have learned to regulate their emotions by minimizing your own. Pleasing others became your way to feel needed, valued, or safe.

The Hidden Goal It's Trying to Fulfill:

The people-pleaser's hidden goal is to *maintain connection by keeping others comfortable — even at your own expense.*

Your subconscious still believes: "If I prioritize myself, I might lose love." So you over-give and under-ask. Your success is dimmed so no one else feels threatened. Your needs are minimized to keep peace. And your voice, little by little, disappears.

What It's Costing You:

Chronic people-pleasing depletes your energy, your time, and your clarity. You may wake up one day unsure of what you even want — because your focus has been so attuned to everyone else. You attract relationships and work environments where your over-functioning is expected. And often, the more you give, the less you feel truly seen.

What to Start Noticing or Doing to Shift It:

- Ask yourself: "What do I believe will happen if I disappoint someone?"
- Practice saying no in low-stakes situations. Let discomfort be your teacher — not a stop sign.
- Get in the habit of checking in with your own needs *before* saying yes. Try: "Let me think about it and get back to you."
- Remind yourself: **Love built on sacrifice isn't love — it's survival. You're allowed to be whole and still be loved.**

Try This Exercise:

- Write down three recent situations where you said yes but wanted to say no.
- For each one, ask: *What was I afraid would happen if I said no?*
- Reflect on where in your family dynamic you learned that it was your job to keep others comfortable.
- Then choose one small thing this week you will decline — not out of rebellion, but out of alignment.

You don't have to earn your place anymore. The people who truly love you won't leave just because you stopped disappearing.

4. THE PERFECTIONIST

How It Shows Up in Daily Life:

You set high standards — for everything. Mistakes feel unbearable. You over-prepare, over-edit, or avoid starting at all because it might not be "good enough." You take pride in excellence but secretly feel weighed down by the pressure to get everything right. Even small setbacks can trigger frustration or shame. Success never feels complete… only "acceptable for now."

The Childhood Role It Grew From:

Many perfectionists grew up in environments where love, safety, or approval were linked to performance. You might have been praised only when you excelled or scolded when you fell short. If you were the "responsible one" or the "golden child," perfection became your currency for belonging. And if chaos or criticism was present in your early life, creating order through achievement may have felt like the only way to stay emotionally afloat.

The Hidden Goal It's Trying to Fulfill:

The perfectionist's hidden goal is to *stay emotionally safe by staying flawless.*

It's a subconscious attempt to avoid criticism, rejection, or shame by proving your worth over and over. But no matter how much you do, it's never enough — because what you're really chasing isn't success. You're chasing the feeling that you're finally "okay."

What It's Costing You:

Perfectionism stalls your progress, exhausts your energy, and limits your joy. It creates unrealistic expectations — not just for yourself, but for others — and often leads to burnout, anxiety, or paralysis. You may be seen as accomplished, but inside, you often feel like a fraud, waiting to be exposed for not having it all together.

What to Start Noticing or Doing to Shift It:

- Ask: "What do I believe will happen if I get it wrong?" Then ask: "Where did I first learn that?"
- Challenge the belief that perfection equals worth. Begin seeing mistakes as data, not danger.
- Set deadlines for creative tasks — not to rush, but to release the fear of endlessly polishing.
- Remind yourself: **You're not here to impress — you're here to express. Your humanity is what makes you magnetic.**

Try This Exercise:

- Choose one area where perfection is paralyzing you (work, appearance, parenting, etc.).
- Write down three ways this pressure is limiting your life.

- Then write a "permission slip" to yourself: *I am allowed to show up messy. I am allowed to grow out loud.*
- Post it somewhere visible — not as a gimmick, but as a daily reset.

Finishing Sentence:

You don't need to be perfect to be powerful. The most magnetic version of you is already enough — flaws, edges, and all.

5. THE REBEL (OR RULE-BREAKER)

How It Shows Up in Daily Life:

You resist rules, systems, and expectations — especially if they come from authority figures. You crave freedom and autonomy, often doing the opposite of what's expected just to reclaim a sense of control. You may sabotage opportunities or delay action simply because someone told you how it "should" be done. The rebel in you pushes back — even when it costs you progress.

The Childhood Role It Grew From:

The Rebel often began as the "defiant one" in childhood — not because you wanted to be difficult, but because defiance was how you preserved your sense of self. You may have grown up with overly strict, controlling, or critical caregivers. Pushing back — or doing things your own way — became your emotional survival. It gave you space to breathe in environments where conformity felt suffocating. Your rebellion wasn't disobedience; it was protection.

The Hidden Goal It's Trying to Fulfill:

The rebel's hidden goal is to *maintain a sense of self by rejecting any identity that feels externally imposed.*

Following someone else's structure — even if it serves you — feels like surrendering your individuality. So you stay just far enough outside the lines to feel like you belong to yourself. The cost? You may throw out useful tools, systems, or support just because they resemble old control.

What It's Costing You:

Rebellion becomes its own prison. In trying to avoid being controlled, you may unconsciously control yourself right out of growth, opportunity, or meaningful success. You resist not only limitations — but support. Progress becomes stop-and-go. You crave impact but may push away structure, feedback, or partnerships that could help you achieve it.

What to Start Noticing or Doing to Shift It:

- Ask: "Am I rejecting this because it's wrong for me — or because it reminds me of someone else's control?"
- Notice when your automatic no is actually a disguised yes — and try staying with the discomfort.
- Reframe structure as *sovereignty,* not submission: systems that you choose can actually *free* you.
- Remind yourself: **You're not being controlled by choosing success. You're being called to lead it.**

Try This Exercise:

- Think of one structure (routine, system, mentor, habit) you've resisted.
- Write down what you *fear* that structure will take away from you (freedom, creativity, independence).
- Then write what it might *give* you if you chose it willingly.

- Try engaging with that structure on *your terms* this week — not as a rule, but as a resource.

True freedom isn't doing the opposite — it's knowing you can choose your own direction without fear of losing yourself.

6. THE UNDERACHIEVER

How It Shows Up in Daily Life:

You hold back. You play small, stay quiet, or settle for "good enough" even when you know you're capable of more. You might avoid opportunities for advancement or success, fearing what they'll require of you. You tell yourself you're "not ready yet" or "don't need that much." You may be incredibly gifted — but you rarely let the world see the full extent of your power.

The Childhood Role It Grew From:

The underachiever often grew up in families where success wasn't encouraged — or where standing out felt threatening. Maybe you were told not to "make waves," "get a big head," or outshine a sibling or parent. Perhaps success was mocked, met with jealousy, or punished. Staying small allowed you to remain emotionally safe. It kept you within the unspoken rules of your family's comfort zone.

The Hidden Goal It's Trying to Fulfill:

The underachiever's hidden goal is to *stay connected by staying invisible, unthreatening, or "less than."*

Your subconscious believes that if you become too successful, you'll be judged, resented, or abandoned. So it quietly downshifts your efforts and dims your ambition. You're not sabotaging your goals because you're afraid of failure — you're afraid of what might happen if you succeed.

What It's Costing You:

Underachievement doesn't protect you — it limits you. You may feel bored, restless, or quietly resentful. Life feels smaller than you know it could be. Over time, this pattern can erode self-esteem, trigger imposter syndrome, and rob you of the fulfillment that comes from fully stepping into your purpose.

What to Start Noticing or Doing to Shift It:

- Ask: "What am I afraid success will change about how others see me?"
- Notice if you're shrinking your goals, your voice, or your visibility in conversations, work, or relationships.
- Begin expanding in safe, controlled ways: share your opinion, raise your standards, or pursue something you've postponed.
- Remind yourself: **You don't owe anyone your smallness. Your greatness doesn't abandon people — it invites them to rise.**

Try This Exercise:

- Write down an opportunity or vision you've quietly talked yourself out of.
- List every reason you've told yourself to stay small — and then write where you first heard those messages.
- Imagine what it would feel like to succeed *without guilt or apology*.

- Take one action this week that aligns with the *bigger* version of you — even if it feels vulnerable.

Playing small never kept you safe — it only kept you hidden. Now, it's safe to be seen.

7 THE OVER-GIVER

How It Shows Up in Daily Life:

You're the helper, the supporter, the one others can always count on. You jump in when someone's in crisis, you give even when your tank is empty, and you rarely ask for help yourself. Your identity is tied to being needed. You may feel secretly exhausted or even resentful — but giving feels safer than receiving. Saying yes is automatic. Saying no feels selfish.

The Childhood Role It Grew From:

Over-givers often grew up in homes where being attuned to others' needs was a form of survival. You may have been the emotional caretaker, peacekeeper, or the "strong one" — even as a child. Taking care of others made you feel valuable and gave you a sense of purpose. It may have also been a way to avoid rejection, punishment, or emotional abandonment.

The Hidden Goal It's Trying to Fulfill:

The over-giver's hidden goal is to *secure love and belonging by always being useful, generous, and self-sacrificing.*

Your subconscious may believe: "If I stop giving, I'll stop mattering." So you pour from an empty cup. You offer support even when it costs you your well-being. Deep down, you may fear that if you had needs, others would walk away — or that you wouldn't know who you are without the role of caregiver.

What It's Costing You:

Over-giving disconnects you from your own needs and eventually leads to burnout, imbalance, and emotional depletion. It can create one-sided relationships, invite takers, and block the reciprocal support you deeply deserve. When you over-give, you teach others that your needs don't matter — and eventually, you may start to believe that yourself.

What to Start Noticing or Doing to Shift It:

- Ask: "What am I hoping to feel by giving so much — and what am I afraid will happen if I don't?"
- Practice pausing before saying yes. Buy yourself a moment with: "Let me get back to you on that."
- Create a boundary around your time or energy this week — not to shut others out, but to stay connected to yourself.
- Remind yourself: **You're not valuable because you give. You're valuable, period.**

Try This Exercise:

- Write down three moments from this week where you gave more than you had to give.
- Ask: *What was I hoping that would earn me?*
- Then write down one thing you truly need right now — and brainstorm one way to give that to *yourself*.
- Practice receiving without guilt: say yes to help, praise, rest, or care — and notice how it feels.

You're allowed to receive as much as you give. You don't need to carry everyone to be worthy of walking beside them.

8. THE NAYSAYER

How It Shows Up in Daily Life:

You see the downside first. Your mind jumps to what could go wrong, how something might fail, or why it probably won't work. You're cautious, skeptical, and tend to poke holes in ideas — especially your own. Optimism can feel naïve or even dangerous. You might label yourself "realistic," but deep down, you often feel blocked by your own doubt.

The Childhood Role It Grew From:

The Naysayer often grew up in environments where dreaming big wasn't encouraged — or was actively discouraged. You may have witnessed failure, disappointment, or instability and learned early on that it's safer not to expect too much. Perhaps you were taught to "be practical" or "not get your hopes up." Negativity became a form of protection — a way to prepare for the worst so you wouldn't be hurt.

The Hidden Goal It's Trying to Fulfill:

The naysayer's hidden goal is to *stay emotionally safe by avoiding risk, disappointment, or rejection.*

Your subconscious believes that if you expect less, you'll be hurt less. Doubt becomes a shield. You dim your dreams so they can't let you down. But in shielding yourself from pain, you also block the possibility of breakthrough — or joy.

What It's Costing You:

Naysaying doesn't protect your heart — it starves it. Your goals lose momentum. You hold back from bold moves or creative ideas because you talk yourself out of them before they ever begin. People may come to you for "reality checks," but you may quietly envy their courage. Over time, your world can become narrower than it needs to be.

What to Start Noticing or Doing to Shift It:

- Ask: "When did I first learn that hope was dangerous — and whose voice does my doubt sound like?"
- Notice how often you shut down your own ideas before they've had a chance to grow.
- Practice saying "What if it *does* work?" before jumping to why it won't.
- Remind yourself: **Hope isn't a setup — it's a strategy. Courage isn't blind faith — it's informed movement.**

Try This Exercise:

- Think of a dream or idea you've dismissed as "unrealistic."
- Write down the worst-case scenario — then write the best-case.
- For one week, take one small action as if the best case were true.
- Pay attention to how it feels to move with belief instead of defense.

You weren't born a naysayer — you became one to stay safe. But it's safe now to believe again.

9. THE PEOPLE PLEASER

How It Shows Up in Daily Life:

You aim to be agreeable, accommodating, and well-liked. You often say yes when you want to say no. You avoid conflict, try to keep the peace, and put others' needs ahead of your own — even when it costs you. You may struggle to express preferences, set boundaries, or disappoint others, and while others may see you as kind or easygoing, inside you may feel invisible, depleted, or resentful.

The Childhood Role It Grew From:

People pleasers often grew up in environments where love, attention, or stability was conditional. You may have received praise when you were "good" or helpful, and criticism or withdrawal when you asserted yourself. You learned that being agreeable kept you connected — and that saying how you really felt might cause someone to leave, lash out, or stop loving you. So you kept the peace — even at the cost of your own identity.

The Hidden Goal It's Trying to Fulfill:

The people pleaser's hidden goal is to *earn acceptance by being who others want you to be — not who you really are.*

Your subconscious believes: "If I'm honest, I'll be rejected. If I disappoint someone, I'll lose them." So you shape-shift. You edit yourself to maintain harmony, unconsciously prioritizing other people's comfort over your own truth. You stay in relationships, roles, or routines that don't fit because being liked feels safer than being real.

What It's Costing You:

People pleasing creates disconnection — not just from others, but from yourself. You may lose track of your own goals, boundaries, and values. You attract people who expect you to over-give or never say no. Your needs go unmet. Over time, resentment builds — not because others are taking too much, but because you've taught yourself to give everything away.

What to Start Noticing or Doing to Shift It:

- Ask: "What part of me believes I have to earn love instead of receive it freely?"
- Practice saying no in low-stakes situations — and sit with the discomfort instead of rushing to fix it.
- Write down three needs or desires you've been avoiding expressing — and practice voicing one this week.
- Remind yourself: **You're not selfish for choosing yourself. You're worthy even when you're not pleasing anyone.**

Try This Exercise:

- Identify one area where you've said yes out of obligation.
- Write: "What was I afraid would happen if I said no?"
- Now write: "What do *I* actually want?"
- Take one step — however small — that aligns with *your* truth, not someone else's expectation.

Finishing Sentence:

You weren't born to keep others comfortable — you were born to live in your truth. You don't have to earn your worth anymore.

10. THE PERFECTIONIST

How It Shows Up in Daily Life:

You strive for excellence — not just to do well, but to avoid doing anything *less* than flawlessly. Mistakes feel catastrophic. You spend hours overthinking, over-preparing, or obsessing over tiny details. You may procrastinate, not because you're lazy, but because starting feels overwhelming — or because you're afraid the outcome won't be "good enough." To others, you seem high-achieving. Inside, you're under constant pressure.

The Childhood Role It Grew From:

The perfectionist often grew up in environments where love, attention, or approval was linked to performance. You may have been praised for accomplishments but overlooked when you were simply *being*. Maybe you learned that your worth came from achievement — or that mistakes brought criticism or shame. Perfection became your armor: if you did everything right, maybe you'd never be rejected, blamed, or unloved.

The Hidden Goal It's Trying to Fulfill:

The perfectionist's hidden goal is to *avoid emotional pain by controlling outcomes and appearing flawless.*

Your subconscious believes: "If I'm perfect, I'll be safe. If I fail, I'll be humiliated or unloved." So you set impossible standards and pressure yourself to never fall short. This hidden goal isn't really about achievement — it's about staying protected. It's about preventing the shame or isolation you may have once felt when you were vulnerable, messy, or simply human.

What It's Costing You:

Perfectionism is a thief. It steals joy from your accomplishments, spontaneity from your life, and peace from your mind. You may struggle to start projects, finish them, or enjoy them once they're done. Burnout is common. So is self-criticism. Even success can feel hollow — because perfection always moves the goalpost. And you may find yourself chronically unsatisfied, no matter how much you do.

What to Start Noticing or Doing to Shift It:

- Ask: "What would happen if I allowed something to be *good enough* instead of perfect?"
- Notice how perfectionism shows up in your language — words like "should," "must," or "have to."
- Allow space for being human: make a small mistake on purpose and sit with the discomfort.
- Remind yourself: **Perfection isn't connection. Being real is what opens the door to love, freedom, and success.**

Try This Exercise:

- Choose one area where perfectionism is holding you back.
- Write down the worst-case scenario of doing it imperfectly — then the *realistic* one.
- Create a "permission slip" for yourself: "I give myself permission to..."
- Take one imperfect action — and celebrate yourself for doing it anyway.

Perfection was your shield — but it's not your freedom. You don't need to be flawless to be phenomenal.

11. THE AVOIDER

How It Shows Up in Daily Life:

You tend to delay, dodge, or distract yourself from uncomfortable tasks, conversations, or decisions. You may keep busy with things that feel easier — like scrolling, cleaning, helping others, or doing "just one more thing" — while avoiding what really needs your attention. Conflict feels unbearable. Deadlines sneak up. You tell yourself you'll deal with it later... but later rarely feels any easier.

The Childhood Role It Grew From:

Avoiders often grew up in environments where expressing emotion, confronting tension, or asserting needs led to rejection, punishment, or chaos. You may have learned that silence was safer than speaking up — or that numbing out was easier than feeling overwhelmed. Avoidance became a survival tool: if you could sidestep discomfort, maybe you could avoid being hurt, judged, or abandoned.

The Hidden Goal It's Trying to Fulfill:

The avoider's hidden goal is to *maintain emotional safety by staying away from discomfort, challenge, or vulnerability.*

Your subconscious believes: "If I don't face it, I won't feel it — and if I don't feel it, I can stay in control." But in avoiding the hard stuff, you also delay growth, truth, and resolution. What began as protection becomes paralysis. You stay stuck — not because you're weak, but because your nervous system is trying to keep you safe.

What It's Costing You:

Avoidance creates long-term stress to escape short-term discomfort. You may struggle with unfinished projects, unresolved relationships, or growing to-do lists. Opportunities pass you by while you wait to feel ready. You become disconnected from your own agency. And ironically, the very things you avoid become the things that weigh on you the most.

What to Start Noticing or Doing to Shift It:

- Ask: "What am I actually afraid will happen if I face this — and when did I first feel that way?"
- Notice what you tend to do *instead* of the thing you're avoiding. That's where your coping lives.
- Practice "micro-exposure": take one tiny action toward the uncomfortable task — and stop there.
- Remind yourself: **You can do hard things in small doses. Avoiding pain often creates more of it.**

Try This Exercise:

- Identify one thing you've been putting off. Write down what it *represents* emotionally.
- Break it into the smallest next step possible — then do just that one thing today.
- Afterward, journal: *How did that feel? What did I fear… and what actually happened?*
- Keep a running list of avoided things you've faced — proof that you're stronger than you feel.

Finishing Sentence:

You don't need to be fearless to move forward — you just need to take one honest step at a time.

12. THE OVER-ANALYZER

How It Shows Up in Daily Life:

You constantly dissect conversations, decisions, or future possibilities — often long after the moment has passed. You replay what was said (or not said), anticipate all possible outcomes, and struggle to make choices because you're caught in a cycle of *"what if...?"* You may feel mentally exhausted, unsure, or stuck — not because you're lazy, but because your brain is working overtime trying to prevent something from going wrong.

The Childhood Role It Grew From:

Over-analyzers often grew up in households where unpredictability, criticism, or emotional instability was the norm. You may have felt responsible for others' moods or well-being — walking on eggshells to prevent an outburst or blame. Thinking things through became a way to anticipate danger, avoid mistakes, or keep people happy. Hyper-vigilance became your armor. Your mind became your survival tool — not for curiosity, but for protection.

The Hidden Goal It's Trying to Fulfill:

The over-analyzer's hidden goal is to *control emotional risk by mentally preparing for — or avoiding — every possible outcome.*

Your subconscious believes: "If I think hard enough, I'll figure out the 'right' answer and stay safe." The mind spins through all scenarios in an attempt to eliminate regret, embarrassment, or rejection. But instead of protecting you, it paralyzes you. The mind becomes a loop instead of a launchpad.

What It's Costing You:

Overanalyzing drains your energy and erodes your confidence. You second-guess your own judgment, delay action, and sometimes miss opportunities because you're still "thinking it through." You may feel disconnected from your intuition — or others may experience you as hesitant or indecisive. The result? You remain stuck in thought... and out of alignment with motion.

What to Start Noticing or Doing to Shift It:

- Ask: "What would I do if I trusted myself — just for today?"
- When you notice your mind spinning, pause and breathe into your body. Shift from *thinking* to *feeling*.
- Use a timer: give yourself 10 minutes to consider an issue — and then choose action over rumination.
- Remind yourself: **No decision creates absolute certainty — but taking action creates clarity.**

Try This Exercise:

- Choose one decision you've been overthinking.
- Write down your top three fears if you choose "wrong." Then write the three *most likely* outcomes.
- Now journal: "What is the *best* thing that could happen if I move forward?"
- Take one real-world step in that direction — even a small one. Record how it felt afterward.

Finishing Sentence:

Your mind was trained to scan for danger — but now, it can be taught to trust your wisdom instead. You don't need every answer to take the first step.

13. THE OVER-GIVER

How It Shows Up in Daily Life:

You're the one everyone turns to — the helper, the caretaker, the dependable one. You offer support without being asked, anticipate others' needs, and often take on more than your share. You might downplay your exhaustion or needs, telling yourself, *"They need me more,"* or *"I can handle it."* On the outside, you appear generous and selfless. On the inside, you may feel depleted, unseen, or quietly resentful.

The Childhood Role It Grew From:

Over-givers often grew up in environments where being useful was the surest path to love, safety, or inclusion. You may have learned that meeting others' needs earned praise, attention, or a temporary sense of control in an unpredictable household. Perhaps you cared for younger siblings, managed emotional tension between adults, or felt responsible for a parent's happiness. Giving became your identity — and your insurance policy against abandonment.

The Hidden Goal It's Trying to Fulfill:

The over-giver's hidden goal is to *secure connection and avoid rejection by being indispensable to others.*

Your subconscious believes: "If I'm always helpful, I'll always be needed — and if I'm needed, I won't be left behind." You give, not just out of kindness, but to hold onto your place in the world. To stop giving feels risky — like disappearing or becoming irrelevant. But this hidden goal keeps you locked in relationships where love is conditional, and rest is never earned.

What It's Costing You:

Over-giving disconnects you from your own desires, limits your capacity, and leaves your needs unmet. You may attract relationships where you are valued for what you *do*, not who you *are*. Burnout, resentment, and low-level sadness often simmer beneath the surface. Eventually, you may not even know what you want anymore — only what everyone else needs.

What to Start Noticing or Doing to Shift It:

- Ask: "What am I hoping to receive by giving so much — and where can I give that to myself instead?"
- Notice where you say yes out of guilt or habit. Pause. Practice saying, "Let me get back to you."
- Write a list of your unmet needs. Choose one to honor this week — unapologetically.
- Remind yourself: **Love is not something you have to earn through service. You're worthy without over-delivering.**

Try This Exercise:

- Choose one relationship where you tend to over-give.
- Write: "What would change if I allowed more balance — or received more?"
- Now journal: "What am I afraid would happen if I stopped giving so much?"
- Practice one small act of receiving — and sit with any discomfort that comes up.

Finishing Sentence:

You don't have to earn your place through exhaustion. You belong even when your hands are empty.

14. THE OVERACHIEVER

How It Shows Up in Daily Life:

You're always chasing the next win. The next title. The next milestone. You push yourself harder than most — setting big goals, staying late, taking pride in being the one who "gets it done." Success feels good... but only briefly. Then it's on to the next thing. You often struggle to slow down, and rest feels uncomfortable — even unsafe. Underneath the drive is a quiet, persistent feeling: *I'm only as good as my latest accomplishment.*

The Childhood Role It Grew From:

Overachievers are often born in environments where worth was measured by results. Maybe praise was only given when you performed well, looked perfect, or made others proud. You may have become "the good one," "the responsible one," or "the one who made the family look successful." Excelling became your identity. But not because you were free — because you felt you had to.

The Hidden Goal It's Trying to Fulfill:

The overachiever's hidden goal is to *earn love, safety, or identity through constant external success.*

Your subconscious believes: "If I keep achieving, I'll finally be enough — and no one will leave me." Accomplishment becomes a defense against rejection, invisibility, or emotional emptiness. But the bar keeps moving. And the more you achieve, the more you fear what might happen if you ever stop.

What It's Costing You:

Overachievement can lead to burnout, anxiety, strained relationships, and a deep disconnection from joy. Your worth gets tied to doing — not being. You may struggle to rest without guilt, or feel lost without a measurable goal. Fulfillment becomes elusive because you've built a life of performance… not presence. And the fear of failure or stillness becomes louder than your own truth.

What to Start Noticing or Doing to Shift It:

- Ask: "Who am I when I'm not achieving?" Then ask again: "Do I like that person?"
- Give yourself permission to rest without reward. Practice doing something *unproductive* on purpose.
- Identify the fear underneath your ambition — and offer that part of you compassion instead of criticism.
- Remind yourself: **You were always worthy — not because of what you've done, but because of who you are.**

Try This Exercise:

- Write: "What does success mean to *me* — not what I was taught?"
- List three things that bring fulfillment but have no external reward.
- Choose one to engage in this week. Pay attention to how it feels to be — not just to do.
- Begin tracking not just your accomplishments… but your moments of peace.

When you stop running from the fear of not being enough, you'll find that who you are is already more than enough.

15. THE PEOPLE PLEASER

How It Shows Up in Daily Life:

You say "yes" when you want to say "no." You smile when you're uncomfortable. You avoid making waves, keep things light, and prioritize others' needs over your own. You may apologize often — even when you've done nothing wrong. Deep down, you want to be liked, accepted, and approved of. You may tell yourself, *"It's not a big deal,"* or *"I don't want to upset anyone."* But inside, you often feel frustrated, invisible, or disconnected from your truth.

The Childhood Role It Grew From:

People pleasers often came from families where love felt conditional — given when you behaved, performed, or kept the peace. You may have learned early that being "good" was safer than being honest. If you made others happy, you were less likely to be criticized, rejected, or blamed. Pleasing others became your way to belong — even if it meant abandoning yourself.

The Hidden Goal It's Trying to Fulfill:

The people pleaser's hidden goal is to *maintain connection and avoid rejection by making others comfortable — at your own expense.*

Your subconscious believes: "If they're happy, I'm safe." So you become hyper-attuned to others' moods, preferences, and expectations — and shape-shift to meet them. It's not manipulation. It's survival. But over time, it disconnects you from your own wants, needs, and sense of self.

What It's Costing You:

People pleasing leads to self-silencing, resentment, and emotional burnout. You may feel like others don't really know the real you — because you rarely show up fully. Boundaries are hard to set (and harder to enforce). You become more responsible for others' feelings than your own fulfillment. And without even realizing it, you start to disappear from your own life.

What to Start Noticing or Doing to Shift It:

- Ask: "Am I saying yes to avoid discomfort — or because I truly want to?"
- Practice small acts of self-expression — even if they make others uncomfortable.
- Notice where you shrink, smooth, or silence yourself. Then gently lean into honesty.
- Remind yourself: **True connection requires truth. People who love you don't need you to be perfect — they need you to be real.**

Try This Exercise:

- Write: "Where in my life am I pleasing instead of honoring myself?"
- Choose one area and write down what you *actually* want or feel.
- Say it out loud — even if just to yourself at first.
- Begin practicing one small "honest no" or "authentic yes" each week.

Finishing Sentence:

You don't need to be liked by everyone — just by the people who truly see you.

16. THE PERFECTIONIST

How It Shows Up in Daily Life:

You hold yourself to impossibly high standards — and you expect the same from others. Your work is never quite "done," and even your accomplishments feel like they could've been better. You often delay finishing things because they're not "ready yet." Mistakes feel like failures. You may appear highly capable, but inside, there's pressure, anxiety, and an underlying fear of being exposed as "not good enough."

The Childhood Role It Grew From:

Perfectionists often grew up in environments where love, praise, or safety was linked to performance. You might've received approval when you succeeded — and criticism, silence, or rejection when you didn't. Some perfectionists had chaotic or emotionally unpredictable upbringings, and controlling outcomes became a form of emotional security. You learned that if you did everything *just right,* maybe nothing would go wrong — and maybe you'd be safe, accepted, or admired.

The Hidden Goal It's Trying to Fulfill:

The perfectionist's hidden goal is to *control how others see you — in order to stay safe, valuable, or emotionally protected.*

Your subconscious believes: "If I can do everything perfectly, I won't be judged, rejected, or hurt." Striving for flawlessness becomes a shield — not for pride, but for protection. The goal isn't excellence... it's avoidance of vulnerability. But this pursuit of perfection creates a loop of never-enough.

What It's Costing You:

Perfectionism robs you of joy, spontaneity, and peace. It delays progress, distorts self-worth, and makes it hard to receive love unless you feel you've "earned" it. It can strain relationships (because nothing ever feels good enough) — and block creativity (because taking risks means tolerating imperfection). It's exhausting. And it's isolating.

What to Start Noticing or Doing to Shift It:

- Ask: "What am I afraid would happen if I let this be imperfect?"
- Challenge yourself to complete something at 80% — and release it anyway.
- Notice when you self-criticize and ask: "Would I speak to a friend this way?"
- Remind yourself: **People don't connect to your polish. They connect to your presence.**

Try This Exercise:

- Write down one area where perfectionism holds you back (work, appearance, parenting, etc.).
- List what *you believe* perfection would protect you from.
- Now list what perfection has cost you — time, peace, relationships, authenticity.
- Commit to one action this week that embraces "done" over "perfect."

Finishing Sentence:

Perfection isn't the path to being loved — it's the wall that keeps love from reaching you.

17. THE AVOIDER

How It Shows Up in Daily Life:

You put things off — not just tasks, but conversations, decisions, and uncomfortable truths. You delay the doctor's appointment, the financial check-in, the tough discussion with your partner or boss. You distract yourself with TV, busywork, scrolling, or planning something else. You may tell yourself, *"It'll work itself out,"* or *"I'll deal with it later."* But deep down, there's a nagging anxiety about what's being left undone.

The Childhood Role It Grew From:

Avoiders often grew up in emotionally overwhelming or unpredictable environments. You may have learned early on that confrontation led to conflict, that expressing needs led to shame, or that facing hard truths made you feel unsafe or unsupported. So you adapted. You learned to shut down, to delay, to minimize, or to escape. Avoidance was your armor. And for a child — it worked.

The Hidden Goal It's Trying to Fulfill:

The avoider's hidden goal is to *maintain emotional safety by staying away from anything that feels too risky, confrontational, or overwhelming.*

Your subconscious believes: "If I don't face it, I can't be hurt by it." Avoidance becomes a survival tool — helping you feel in control when the world feels too much. But while it protects you from short-term discomfort, it keeps you stuck in long-term limitation.

What It's Costing You:

Avoidance creates anxiety, confusion, and stagnation. The things you push away don't disappear—they grow heavier. Procrastinated conversations become resentment. Ignored finances become crisis. Delayed decisions become missed opportunities. It quietly erodes your confidence, your clarity, and your ability to move forward. You stop trusting yourself to handle life.

What to Start Noticing or Doing to Shift It:

- Ask: "What am I *really* afraid will happen if I face this?"
- Choose one small, non-threatening thing you've been avoiding — and take action today.
- Remind yourself: discomfort is temporary, but avoidance creates lasting pain.
- Use this mantra: **"I can handle hard things. Avoidance is no longer my protector — awareness is."**

Try This Exercise:

- Write: "What do I tend to avoid most — and what has it cost me?"
- Journal about a time you avoided something and it created more pain — then a time you faced something and grew stronger.
- Choose one small truth to face this week — and write out the best possible outcome if you address it.
- Then go do it. Don't wait for confidence. Let clarity be the thing you practice.

Avoidance may have protected you once — but now, facing the truth is the very thing that sets you free.

18. THE MARTYR

How It Shows Up in Daily Life:

You give endlessly. You say yes when you're exhausted. You pick up the slack. You put everyone else's needs first and wear your selflessness like a badge of honor. But deep down, there's a quiet ache — a feeling that no one sees how much you give, or how much it costs you. You may feel overworked, underappreciated, and quietly resentful. And yet, when someone offers to help… you often say, *"It's okay, I've got it."*

The Childhood Role It Grew From:

Martyrs often grew up in households where their needs were secondary — or punished. You may have been the responsible one, the emotional caretaker, the peacekeeper. You learned early that your value came from what you did for others, not who you were. Love, approval, or safety may have been tied to your willingness to sacrifice — so you made it your identity.

The Hidden Goal It's Trying to Fulfill:

The martyr's hidden goal is to *secure belonging and significance through self-sacrifice.*

Your subconscious believes: "If I give enough, they'll love me. If I keep proving my worth, I won't be left behind." Giving becomes a strategy for survival — not out of pure generosity, but out of a deep-rooted belief that you must *earn* your place in people's lives. But you can never give enough to feel truly filled.

What It's Costing You:

Martyrdom often leads to depletion, burnout, and resentment. You may feel invisible in your relationships — yet afraid to stop giving, in case it means losing connection. Your boundaries blur. Your own desires become unknown even to you. And over time, the people you love may come to expect your sacrifice — without realizing it's costing you your sense of self.

What to Start Noticing or Doing to Shift It:

- Ask: "What part of me believes I have to earn love by giving everything away?"
- Practice receiving. Let someone else take the lead. Say yes to being supported.
- Recognize that your value is not in what you provide — it's in who you *are*.
- Use this truth: **"Sacrifice that silences me isn't noble — it's abandonment of self."**

Try This Exercise:

- Write: "What are the things I do out of obligation — not true desire?"
- Choose one recurring pattern and ask yourself, "If I didn't do this... what would I fear happening?"
- Then write: "What might actually happen if I stop doing it?"
- Begin experimenting with saying no in one area — and notice how it feels to keep your energy for yourself.

When you stop giving from depletion and start giving from alignment, your love becomes more powerful — and your life, more your own.

19. THE CONTROLLER

How It Shows Up in Daily Life:

You need things done a certain way — your way. You struggle to delegate. You get anxious when things feel out of your hands, and you often take charge just to ease that internal tension. You may feel like others slow you down or can't be trusted to get things right. You feel most safe when you're the one steering the ship. But beneath the surface, control isn't about power — it's about protection.

The Childhood Role It Grew From:

Controllers often grew up in chaotic, inconsistent, or emotionally unstable households. Maybe the adults in your life weren't reliable — so you learned early to rely only on yourself. Perhaps you were forced to take on adult responsibilities before you were ready. Control became your lifeline. It was how you brought order to an unpredictable world — and how you avoided being blindsided, hurt, or forgotten.

The Hidden Goal It's Trying to Fulfill:

The controller's hidden goal is to *prevent pain, disappointment, or rejection by staying in charge of outcomes and emotions.*

Your subconscious believes: "If I'm in control, nothing can catch me off guard — and I won't be hurt." You don't necessarily want to dominate others; you just want to minimize risk. But this protective drive creates constant pressure, loneliness, and a fear of vulnerability — because letting go feels like letting danger in.

What It's Costing You:

Living in control mode leads to exhaustion and disconnection. Relationships become strained — people may feel micromanaged, dismissed, or untrusted. You carry more than your share, but don't trust others to help. You miss out on the richness that comes with surrender, flow, and emotional intimacy. You may achieve a lot — but it often feels hollow, because you're doing it all alone.

What to Start Noticing or Doing to Shift It:
- Ask: "What am I afraid will happen if I'm not in control of this?"
- Notice moments of tension in your body when something unexpected happens — and pause before reacting.
- Practice trusting others with small responsibilities. Let things be imperfect.
- Use this reminder: **"Control keeps me safe, but surrender sets me free."**

Try This Exercise:
- Write: "Where in my life do I over-function because I don't trust others to follow through?"
- Identify one area (work, family, projects) where you can delegate or release control.
- Reflect on what that control protected you from in the past — and what it's costing you now.
- Begin letting go in micro-moments: pause, breathe, and let it unfold.

Finishing Sentence:

True power comes not from controlling everything — but from trusting yourself to handle whatever unfolds.

20. THE PERFORMER

How It Shows Up in Daily Life:

You know how to charm, impress, and show up looking put-together. People often admire your confidence or charisma — but underneath the polish, there's a fear of being truly seen. You may feel like you're constantly "on," adjusting who you are depending on who's watching. You seek validation through performance — accomplishments, image, accolades — but rarely feel deeply at peace or truly connected.

The Childhood Role It Grew From:

Performers often grew up in environments where love and attention were conditional — awarded for good behavior, achievement, or likability. You might have been praised when you performed well, but ignored or shamed when you were simply *yourself*. So you learned: if I shine, they'll notice me. If I impress them, they'll want me. Being yourself wasn't safe — but performing earned connection.

The Hidden Goal It's Trying to Fulfill:

The performer's hidden goal is to *earn love and belonging through visibility, success, and admiration.*

Your subconscious believes: "If I can just impress them enough, they'll never leave me. If I keep performing, they won't see the parts of me I'm afraid to show." So you chase applause — not out of arrogance, but out of longing. Yet no performance ever feels like enough, because what you truly crave is to be loved *without the mask.*

What It's Costing You:

Performance keeps you disconnected — from others and from yourself. You may feel isolated, even in a crowd. Relationships stay surface-level, because you don't reveal your real thoughts or vulnerabilities. You're always "on," always striving — and rarely feel safe enough to exhale. It's hard to rest when your identity feels tied to how well you're received.

What to Start Noticing or Doing to Shift It:

- Ask: "When do I feel the need to perform, rather than just be present?"
- Notice when you adjust your behavior to gain approval — and pause to check in with your authentic self.
- Begin small acts of honesty: say what you really feel, even if it risks disapproval.
- Use this truth: **"The love I'm seeking won't come from impressing — it comes from being."**

Try This Exercise:

- Journal about a time you performed for love — and a time you were loved without performing.
- Write: "What do I fear people would think if I stopped trying to impress them?"
- Practice showing up this week without the polish: speak truthfully, show a flaw, or share something vulnerable.
- Reflect afterward on how it felt — and what actually happened.

You don't have to earn your worth through performance — you were worthy long before the spotlight.

21. THE DOUBTER

How It Shows Up in Daily Life:

You second-guess everything. Decisions take forever. You over-research, overanalyze, and ask others for constant reassurance — but you still don't trust your gut. Even when things go well, you wonder if you got lucky. You may quietly question your own abilities, value, or instincts. Self-doubt follows you like a shadow, and though others may see your strengths, you often feel like you're one wrong move away from being exposed.

The Childhood Role It Grew From:

Doubters often grew up in families where confidence was discouraged — or where criticism came faster than support. Maybe you were shamed for speaking up, told you were wrong when you weren't, or constantly compared to someone "better." You may have learned that your voice wasn't important or that mistakes were dangerous. Over time, you internalized the idea that it's safer not to trust yourself — and to always check with someone else first.

The Hidden Goal It's Trying to Fulfill:

The doubter's hidden goal is to *stay emotionally safe by avoiding risks, mistakes, or rejection through constant hesitation and self-questioning.*

Your subconscious believes: "If I doubt myself, I won't overstep. If I stay small and uncertain, I won't get hurt or humiliated." Doubt becomes a protective barrier — keeping you from leaping forward, but also from truly living.

What It's Costing You:

Self-doubt erodes confidence, clarity, and forward momentum. Opportunities slip by while you're still "thinking about it." You hold yourself back, talk yourself out of possibilities, and stay stuck in loops of second-guessing. It's exhausting — and lonely — to feel like you can't even trust your own instincts. You begin to depend too heavily on others to define your worth or your next step.

What to Start Noticing or Doing to Shift It:

- Ask: "Whose voice does my doubt sound like — and is it still true today?"
- Start celebrating *evidence* of your own wisdom: things you got right, risks that worked out.
- Make one decision this week without polling anyone else — and trust yourself to navigate it.
- Use this shift: **"Doubt is a learned habit — not a life sentence."**

Try This Exercise:

- Journal: "What do I regularly doubt about myself — and what has that hesitation cost me?"
- List three times you made a decision on your own that turned out well — and what that says about your instincts.
- Set a 24-hour decision rule for low-stakes situations: give yourself permission to act without delay.
- Begin affirming: "I can trust myself — I've earned it."

When you stop outsourcing your confidence, you reclaim the power to lead your life — on your own terms.

22. THE VICTIM

How It Shows Up in Daily Life:

You feel like life keeps happening *to* you. Nothing ever quite works out, no matter how hard you try. You may find yourself frequently saying things like "Just my luck," or "Of course this would happen to me." Challenges feel personal, unfair, and unchangeable. You often feel unsupported, misunderstood, or like others have it easier than you. There's a heaviness — a sense that something outside of you is always getting in the way.

The Childhood Role It Grew From:

Victim patterns often take root in families where a child felt powerless, ignored, or blamed unfairly. Perhaps you were punished for things you didn't do, or your emotions were dismissed altogether. You may have been told you were "too sensitive" or made to feel like a burden. If you were rarely protected or advocated for, you may have learned to cope by staying small, helpless, or unseen — silently hoping someone would eventually come rescue you.

The Hidden Goal It's Trying to Fulfill:

The victim's hidden goal is to *avoid disappointment and responsibility by staying in a position of helplessness.*

Your subconscious believes: "If I admit I have power, then I'm responsible for the pain I've experienced — and for what happens next." It's safer, emotionally, to believe the world is against you than to risk believing you *could* change things... and be proven wrong again. Victimhood becomes a shield against further hurt — but it also keeps you trapped.

What It's Costing You:

When you view yourself as powerless, you unconsciously give up opportunities for growth, change, and self-trust. You stay stuck in cycles of blame or self-pity. Others may pull away over time, unsure how to support you. Most of all, you begin to believe your story of limitation — and act from it, reinforcing it, again and again.

What to Start Noticing or Doing to Shift It:

- Ask: "What do I gain by staying in the 'this always happens to me' mindset?"
- Practice separating *what happened* from *what you made it mean.*
- Begin looking for moments, even small ones, where you had more agency than you thought.
- Use this new truth: **"My past may explain me — but it doesn't have to define me."**

Try This Exercise:

- Journal: "Where in my life do I feel the most powerless — and what is that story protecting me from?"
- Choose one area and write: "If I did believe I had some power here, what might I do next?"
- Take a single small step in that direction — and observe the result.
- Begin reframing: "This happened... *but now I get to decide what I do with it.*"

Reclaiming your power doesn't mean denying your pain — it means choosing not to live from it anymore.

24. THE ISOLATOR

How It Shows Up in Daily Life:

You prefer to handle things alone. You rarely ask for help, even when you're overwhelmed. You may avoid social invitations, delay replying to texts, or find reasons not to open up emotionally — even to the people closest to you. You might tell yourself you're just "independent," but deep down, there's a fear of being seen too closely or being let down if you let others in. Connection feels risky — so distance becomes your default.

The Childhood Role It Grew From:

Isolators often grew up in environments where vulnerability led to pain. You may have been betrayed, shamed, or ignored when you needed support. You might've been the "strong one" — the one who wasn't allowed to cry, fall apart, or need anything. Over time, you learned that opening up only led to disappointment. So you created safety by building emotional walls and depending only on yourself.

The Hidden Goal It's Trying to Fulfill:

The isolator's hidden goal is to *avoid emotional risk, rejection, or disappointment by staying self-contained and emotionally unavailable.*

Your subconscious believes: "If I don't need anyone, I can't be hurt. If I stay separate, no one can reject me." Isolation becomes armor — protecting your heart, but also keeping it lonely. You may crave closeness, yet sabotage it the moment it gets real.

What It's Costing You:

Staying isolated cuts off the very support, love, and intimacy you long for. You might find success professionally, but personal fulfillment feels just out of reach. Relationships remain surface-level or one-sided. You end up exhausted from doing everything alone — and resentful, even though you've pushed people away. The loneliness you feel is real... but so is the possibility of healing it.

What to Start Noticing or Doing to Shift It:

- Ask: "Where did I first learn that it wasn't safe to need anyone?"
- Begin with small emotional disclosures: share a thought, a fear, or a vulnerable truth.
- Allow someone to help you this week, even in a minor way.
- Repeat this truth: **"Letting others in doesn't make me weak — it makes me real."**

Try This Exercise:

- Journal: "What do I fear would happen if I truly let someone in?"
- Reflect on the people in your life — who has earned a deeper version of you?
- Choose one person and share something honest you've been withholding.
- Track how it feels to let yourself be seen — even if just a little more.

Finishing Sentence:

The walls you built once kept you safe — but now, they may be keeping everything you long for out.

25. THE PROVER

How It Shows Up in Daily Life:

You're constantly trying to prove yourself — often without realizing it. Achievements aren't just accomplishments; they're validations. You may overwork, overdeliver, or overcommit in hopes that someone — anyone — will finally acknowledge your worth. Even after a success, you quickly move on to the next goal, hungry for more evidence that you're enough. You're driven, but often exhausted. Deep down, it never quite feels like you've "arrived."

The Childhood Role It Grew From:

Provers usually grew up in households where love was conditional — where praise, approval, or attention had to be *earned*. Maybe success got you noticed. Maybe failure brought shame or silence. You may have learned that being valued meant being valuable. So you became the achiever, the golden child, the one who got things done. Your identity fused with your performance — and slowing down felt like disappearing.

The Hidden Goal It's Trying to Fulfill:

The prover's hidden goal is to *earn love, safety, or belonging by constantly producing, achieving, or impressing.*

Your subconscious believes: "If I stop proving myself, I'll stop mattering. If I don't excel, I'll be invisible or rejected." You've been running not just toward success — but away from the terrifying idea that you're not enough *as you are.*

What It's Costing You:

Living in proving mode keeps you disconnected from your true self. You might feel admired but not deeply known. You may attract opportunities but feel no joy in them. Burnout becomes a lifestyle. Worst of all, you never truly feel *safe* — because your sense of worth depends on constant doing. You don't know how to be enough without performing.

What to Start Noticing or Doing to Shift It:

- Ask: "Who am I trying to prove this to — and when did I first learn I had to?"
- Begin noticing your worth apart from what you achieve.
- Allow yourself to rest or say no without explanation — and watch what stories surface.
- Use this new truth: **"I don't have to earn what I already am."**

Try This Exercise:

- Journal: "If I never had to prove anything again, how would I live differently?"
- Write a list of qualities you love in others that have nothing to do with success.
- Reflect: "What if those qualities are also what make *me* lovable?"
- Practice stillness — and notice what comes up when you're not in motion.

Finishing Sentence:

You were never meant to prove your worth — only to remember it.

26. THE CHAMELEON

How It Shows Up in Daily Life:

You change depending on who you're around. You can read the room instantly and adapt — smoothing conflict, agreeing outwardly, shifting tone or personality to match the crowd. You're likable, agreeable, and well-received... but often unsure of who you *really* are underneath. Your wants and needs are blurry, and you may second-guess yourself constantly. You blend in so well that even you forget what feels true for you.

The Childhood Role It Grew From:

Chameleons are often raised in households where being authentic felt risky — maybe emotions weren't welcome, or you had to walk on eggshells around volatile or demanding parents. You may have learned that being accepted required you to shape-shift: be quieter, nicer, more agreeable, less *you*. In families with chaos or unpredictability, being attuned to others' moods and becoming who they needed was a survival strategy.

The Hidden Goal It's Trying to Fulfill:

The chameleon's hidden goal is to *maintain connection and avoid rejection by constantly adjusting to others' expectations.*

Your subconscious believes: "If I become who they want, I won't be abandoned. If I express the real me, I'll be punished or left." You protect yourself by staying invisible — not through distance, but by being *exactly* what others want. But the cost is high.

What It's Costing You:

Over time, you lose sight of your identity. Decisions become difficult. You feel anxious around conflict and unsure of your opinions. You might find yourself overcommitting, people-pleasing, or quietly resenting others for not knowing what you *really* want — even though you've never told them. Your authenticity becomes the price you pay for acceptance.

What to Start Noticing or Doing to Shift It:

- Ask: "Where am I saying yes when I mean no?"
- Practice expressing small, honest opinions — even if they differ from the group.
- Notice who drains you and who allows you to be your full self.
- Use this mantra: **"I don't have to disappear to be loved."**

Try This Exercise:

- Journal: "When in my life did I learn it wasn't okay to be fully myself?"
- Write down five things you *actually* want this week — even if no one else wants them.
- Choose one and act on it, even if it feels uncomfortable.
- Reflect afterward: Did anything terrible happen — or did I survive being seen?

Finishing Sentence:

You don't have to shape-shift to belong — the right people will stay when the real you shows up.

27. THE SHADOW COMPETITOR

How It Shows Up in Daily Life:

You don't always admit it, but you constantly compare yourself to others. Whether it's social media, coworkers, friends, or even strangers, you measure where you stand. You might feel quietly superior one moment and deeply inadequate the next. You downplay others' success to feel okay — or overinflate theirs and shrink yourself in response. You may never call it "competition," but you always keep score. And when others succeed, a part of you feels unseen or left behind.

The Childhood Role It Grew From:

The shadow competitor often came from a family where love or approval was tied to comparison. Maybe a sibling was the "golden child," or you were compared to others in subtle, biting ways: "Why can't you be more like...?" Maybe your achievements were overlooked while someone else's were celebrated. You internalized the idea that life is a ranking — and that your worth depends on winning, outperforming, or at least *not losing*.

The Hidden Goal It's Trying to Fulfill:

The shadow competitor's hidden goal is to *stay emotionally significant by outperforming others or avoiding falling behind*.

Your subconscious believes: "If I'm not ahead, I'm forgotten. If they win, I disappear." The competition isn't really about others — it's about desperately trying to stay connected, valued, and visible in a world that once made you feel replaceable.

What It's Costing You:

Comparison keeps you from peace. It turns others into threats, and success into a zero-sum game. You may sabotage relationships, withhold support, or constantly shift your goals just to "keep up." Worst of all, it disconnects you from your true desires — because your motivation becomes about not losing rather than genuinely thriving. You chase validation instead of fulfillment.

What to Start Noticing or Doing to Shift It:

- Ask: "When did I first feel like I had to compete to matter?"
- Celebrate someone else's win this week — and notice what feelings it brings up.
- Reconnect to your own goals: what would you want *if no one else existed to compare to?*
- Remind yourself: **"Someone else's light doesn't dim mine."**

Try This Exercise:

- Journal: "Who do I compare myself to the most — and what does their success trigger in me?"
- Write down 5 things that make *you* successful beyond external achievements.
- List 3 moments where you felt proud — and explore why they mattered to *you*, not others.
- Practice sending silent support to someone you envy — and notice how it shifts your energy.

You don't need to compete to count — your worth isn't measured against anyone else's.

28. THE OVERCOMMITTER

How It Shows Up in Daily Life:

Your calendar is overflowing. You say yes before thinking, take on more than you can manage, and constantly find yourself running behind or stretched thin. You may feel responsible for everyone's needs — at work, at home, in your community. You're the reliable one, the "go-to," the one who *never drops the ball*... even when you're falling apart inside. Slowing down feels selfish. Saying no feels dangerous. So you keep piling it on — even when it's quietly breaking you down.

The Childhood Role It Grew From:

Over-committers often grew up in families where their value came from what they did for others. Maybe you were the helper, the caretaker, the peacekeeper — the one who held everything together. You might've had to grow up fast, managing adult responsibilities as a child. Your worth became linked to service, to being useful, to being "the strong one." Rest wasn't modeled, and boundaries may not have been respected. You learned early that love came at the cost of your own needs.

The Hidden Goal It's Trying to Fulfill:

The over-committer's hidden goal is to *maintain connection and self-worth by constantly proving usefulness and reliability.*

Your subconscious believes: "If I stop doing, I'll stop mattering. If I say no, I'll be abandoned." Every yes is a way to avoid the unbearable feeling of being unwanted or unseen. You're not just trying to help — you're trying to belong.

What It's Costing You:

Overcommitting depletes your energy, fogs your purpose, and leads to resentment. You may start to feel used, overlooked, or invisible — especially when others don't reciprocate. But the truth is, you trained them to expect it. You lose time, space, and the opportunity to hear your own voice. Eventually, you burn out... or silently implode.

What to Start Noticing or Doing to Shift It:

- Ask: "Who taught me that my needs were less important than others'?"
- Pause before saying yes — and give yourself time to decide.
- Say no to something small this week and track what happens (spoiler: probably nothing terrible).
- Repeat this truth: **"Saying no isn't rejection — it's self-respect."**

Try This Exercise:

- Journal: "Where do I overextend myself the most — and why?"
- List 3 things you've said yes to recently that you wish you hadn't.
- For each, ask: What was I afraid would happen if I said no?
- Practice setting one clear boundary this week — and honor it.

Finishing Sentence:

You don't have to do it all to deserve it all — your worth was never meant to be earned through exhaustion.

29. THE DISAPPOINTER

How It Shows Up in Daily Life:

You expect to let people down — and sometimes, you do. You might forget appointments, show up late, miss deadlines, or underdeliver... even when you deeply *want* to do well. There's a sense of dread around follow-through, as if something inside is resisting success. You may even sabotage things at the last minute — a job interview, a relationship, a presentation — and afterward, feel both ashamed and oddly familiar with the outcome. Like part of you always knew it would go that way.

The Childhood Role It Grew From:

Disappointers often came from environments where they were *expected* to fail. Maybe you were criticized more than praised. Maybe you were constantly reminded of your flaws, or felt you could never live up to expectations. Eventually, you adopted the role of the "letdown" — not because it felt good, but because it was *predictable*. At least if you failed, no one would be surprised. You beat them to the punch. And deep down, part of you learned: "If I disappoint first, I won't be blindsided by rejection later."

The Hidden Goal It's Trying to Fulfill:

The disappointer's hidden goal is to *avoid the pain of unexpected rejection or failure by sabotaging success preemptively.*

Your subconscious believes: "If I mess it up myself, it'll hurt less than if someone else does it to me. If I don't rise too high, I won't fall." The identity of "the one who doesn't quite deliver" becomes a shield against disappointment — even as it keeps you small.

What It's Costing You:

Living this pattern chips away at your self-trust and reputation. Opportunities pass you by. People stop relying on you. You may feel constantly misunderstood — as if others don't see your good intentions, only your missed steps. But the real cost is internal: You stop believing in your potential. You assume you're destined to underperform. And that becomes your ceiling.

What to Start Noticing or Doing to Shift It:

- Ask: "What was said about me growing up — and have I internalized those stories?"
- Acknowledge one area where you're afraid to succeed, and why.
- Complete one small thing you've been putting off — not to prove anything, but to reclaim your agency.
- Use this affirmation: **"I'm not here to live down to anyone's expectations — not even my own."**

Try This Exercise:

- Journal: "Who was disappointed in me — and when did I start expecting myself to fail?"
- Write a letter (not to send) to someone whose criticism shaped your identity.
- Finish this sentence 5 times: "If I believed I couldn't disappoint anyone, I would…"
- Choose one of those and take a bold step toward it this week.

You are not your past pattern — you're the author of your future outcome, no longer defined by who others expected you to be.

30. THE INVISIBLE ONE

How It Shows Up in Daily Life:

You keep a low profile. You hesitate to speak up in groups, rarely share your opinions unless asked, and often feel like others overlook or talk over you. You may avoid drawing attention to yourself — not because you lack value, but because somewhere deep down, you feel safer staying unseen. You might deflect compliments, minimize your accomplishments, or wait for permission to step forward... even though a part of you aches to be recognized, valued, and heard.

The Childhood Role It Grew From:

Invisible ones often grew up in households where being quiet was praised or required — or where being seen came with risk. You may have learned to fly under the radar to avoid punishment, criticism, or conflict. Maybe the loudest or most demanding family member took up all the space, leaving you to shrink. Perhaps you were labeled the "easy one," the "good kid," or just simply... not noticed. Over time, you learned that invisibility was safety — and visibility was vulnerability.

The Hidden Goal It's Trying to Fulfill:

The invisible one's hidden goal is to *maintain emotional safety by avoiding attention, scrutiny, or disapproval.*

Your subconscious believes: "If no one sees me, they can't reject me. If I don't take up space, I won't be a problem." Remaining unseen becomes a protective layer that preserves connection by avoiding disruption — even if it costs you your voice.

What It's Costing You:

Staying invisible silences your contributions, your dreams, and your leadership. Opportunities pass you by. Relationships feel one-sided. You begin to question whether your presence even matters. Over time, this creates quiet despair — a life of playing small not because you lack the talent, but because you've been conditioned to believe that visibility is unsafe. It's not that you don't have brilliance... it's that you've hidden it too well.

What to Start Noticing or Doing to Shift It:

- Ask: "When did I learn that being seen was risky?"
- Speak up once this week when you normally wouldn't — even if your voice shakes.
- Acknowledge a recent win out loud (to a friend, or even to yourself).
- Use this mantra: **"I am safe to be seen, and I matter when I show up."**

Try This Exercise:

- Journal: "What was my family's attitude toward attention and visibility?"
- Write down three ways you've played small in the last month — and what you wish you'd done differently.
- Practice taking up space: stand tall, breathe deeply, and visualize yourself confidently entering a room.
- Each day this week, take one small action that affirms: *I am here, and I count.*

You were never meant to disappear — the world needs the version of you that finally dares to be visible.

By using these exercises you can start Reclaiming the Power Behind the Patterns

Now that you've met the saboteurs, you've done something most people never do — you've looked directly at the unconscious patterns that shape your thoughts, your choices, and your results.

That's no small thing.

These patterns were never random. Each one was built for a reason — to help you stay connected, accepted, and emotionally safe in the only way your younger self knew how. But now, you're no longer that child. You have more power, more perspective, and more possibility than ever before.

Recognizing your saboteurs doesn't mean judging them. It means **freeing yourself** from their grip. It means reclaiming the parts of you that have been buried under old survival strategies. It means aligning your conscious goals with a subconscious that no longer needs to sabotage them in order to feel safe.

And it goes even deeper.

Understanding these patterns doesn't *just* change how you treat yourself — it changes how you see others. In the next chapter You begin to recognize the fears behind their behaviors. The roles they still think they need to play. The stories they don't even realize they're living out. This kind of insight creates compassion. It builds bridges where there were once walls. It softens judgment and replaces it with connection.

The better you understand your own patterns, the more clearly you'll see the truth in others. And that clarity makes everything — relationships, careers, confidence, and fulfillment — so much easier to navigate.

So, take a moment.

Let it land: **You're not broken. You've been patterned.**

But now, you're aware.

And awareness is what changes everything.

In the next chapter you will see your awareness deepen, something unexpected happens — you stop seeing other people's behavior at face value and begin to recognize the hidden patterns, fears, and roles driving them too.

CHAPTER 17

LIFE AFTER THE SHIFT

There comes a moment—sometimes quiet, sometimes profound—when you realize something fundamental has changed. You're not reacting the same way you used to. You're not overthinking, defending, avoiding, or shrinking. You find yourself responding with calm instead of urgency, presence instead of pretense, clarity instead of confusion.

This is the beginning of life after the shift.

You may not be able to pinpoint the exact second it happened. You may not even feel fully settled in your new self yet. But something is different. And as you continue on this path, that difference becomes the new default.

THE SUBTLE ARRIVAL

Living after the shift doesn't always come with fireworks or a triumphant scene. More often, it feels like a series of quiet victories. You make a choice that aligns with your truth instead of your fear. You speak up instead of shrinking back. You give yourself permission to rest without guilt. These small wins add up—and suddenly, you realize you're not who you used to be.

Clients often describe this moment with surprise. One woman who struggled for years with imposter syndrome said, "I was in a meeting, and for the first time, I didn't feel like I was faking anything. I just spoke. It wasn't perfect, but it was mine. And it felt... easy."

Another client, a former perfectionist, told me, "I let my teenager see that I messed up—and instead of spiraling into shame, I laughed. I apologized. I was human. That never used to feel safe."

These are signs of the shift taking root. You're no longer trying to "get there." You realize you already 'are' there—and now you're simply living from that new space.

THE EVOLUTION OF IDENTITY

One of the most profound aspects of this transformation is the evolution of identity. For most people, the person they were before the shift was built around survival strategies—playing the role the family needed, suppressing brilliance to avoid envy, staying small to stay safe. These identities weren't chosen; they were inherited.

But now, after the shift, you get to choose.

This process is tender. **Sometimes, you'll feel like you're straddling two worlds**—the **old identity that still wants to protect you, and the new one that wants to express you**. You may feel unsure at times: 'Am I really allowed to live this way? Can I trust this ease?'

Yes, you can.

You may no longer be the helper who puts everyone else first. You may no longer be the achiever who measures worth by productivity. You may no longer be the invisible one who stays silent to avoid conflict. And when you step out of those identities, people around you will feel it. Some will be uncomfortable. Others will be inspired. But you'll know, deep down, that this is who you really are.

The old identity doesn't need to be destroyed. It simply needs to be honored for the protection it gave—and then gently retired. The new identity isn't a mask. It's the unveiling of what's always been true underneath.

GETTING USED TO THE NEW YOU

Stepping into a new identity doesn't always feel like stepping into a celebration. Sometimes, it feels like inviting a stranger into your home — someone you know is supposed to be there, but you're still learning how to trust.

That's normal.

Even when the shift has happened — even when your patterns have realigned and you've started making new choices — the old identity doesn't vanish overnight. It lingers. It taps on the glass, asking to come back inside. Not because it's evil or broken, but because it's familiar.

You wore that identity for years, maybe decades. It kept you safe. It shaped how you connected with others, how you responded to life, how you saw yourself. And now, even though it no longer fits, it still remembers its way around the house.

But now you have a choice. You can thank it, acknowledge it, and gently keep walking forward — from a different place. You can choose your new self again and again, not with force, but with compassion. Not as an act of war on the past, but as an act of love toward your future.

Welcoming your transformed identity can be awkward at first. You may not know how to *be* this new version of yourself. You may question if it's real. That's okay. Imagine it like getting to know a new roommate: it takes time to understand their rhythms, their boundaries, their voice. But eventually, they feel like home.

You don't need to perform your new identity. You only need to allow it. Live with it. Choose it. And let it reveal itself to you in deeper and deeper ways.

Because you didn't just change your thoughts — you shifted your frequency.

And now, your life will begin to reflect that.

The shift wasn't just intellectual. It was vibrational. Energetic. Foundational.

You didn't just learn new tools — you became someone new. Someone whose inner frequency no longer matches fear, scarcity, or self-betrayal.

And just like a radio dial, once you tune into a new frequency, the static from the old one starts to fade.

Your outer world starts to catch up with your inner transformation — sometimes slowly, sometimes all at once — but inevitably.

You'll begin noticing different conversations showing up. Different people. Different opportunities.

You'll feel more moments of peace where there used to be noise.

More clarity where there used to be confusion.

More self-trust where there used to be doubt.

And even when challenges arise, they won't pull you off course the way they once did.

Why? Because you're no longer trying to live a new life with the energy of the old one.

You're becoming a vibrational match to everything you've been asking for — not by force, but by alignment.

This is where manifestation begins to feel... natural.

Not like a practice, but like a truth.

Because when you live in the frequency of who you really are, life can't help but respond.

Because you didn't just change your thoughts — you shifted your frequency. And now, your life will begin to reflect that.

The old you might whisper, "This won't last."

That's when you whisper back, "This is who I am now."

THE RELATIONSHIP SHIFT

One of the most surprising and rewarding changes after the shift happens in your relationships. Not because the other person changes—but because 'you' do.

When you understand your own patterns, you stop needing others to fix or validate you. You stop playing out the old dances of projection and reactivity. You no longer feel the compulsion to prove your worth or rescue someone from their pain. You can be with people without losing yourself.

Imagine this: You're at a family dinner. A parent or sibling starts to push the same old buttons—but this time, the button isn't there.

You don't take the bait. You smile, stay grounded, maybe even change the subject with kindness. And instead of storming away or shutting down, you stay connected to 'yourself'. That is power. That is peace.

You begin to draw new kinds of people into your life. Aligned people. People who reflect the new frequency you're operating from. Relationships deepen or dissolve naturally—not from drama, but from clarity.

You start to feel safe being seen. And that changes everything.

THE STAGES OF INTEGRATION

It's important to understand that this new way of living doesn't become permanent overnight. It's a process. One you can trust.

Psychologists refer to four stages of learning and integration, and they apply beautifully to this work:

1. "Unconscious Incompetence" – You don't know what you don't know. You're unaware of the patterns running your life.
2. "Conscious Incompetence" – You begin to see the patterns, but you haven't yet shifted them. This stage can feel messy and humbling.
3. "Conscious Competence" – You're able to catch yourself, redirect, and live from a more empowered space—but it still takes effort.
4. "Unconscious Competence" – It becomes second nature. The shift is not something you 'do'. It's who you are.

You'll move through these stages in different areas at different times. Some shifts will come easily. Others may take longer. That's okay. The key is to keep returning to alignment. Over time, you'll spend less time in resistance and more time in flow.

LIVING THE NEW RHYTHM

Success after the shift feels different. It's not about proving, performing, or pushing. It's about allowing, creating, receiving. You don't need to control everything. You don't panic when things go sideways. You trust the timing of your life.

This doesn't mean challenges disappear. But your 'relationship' to them does. You stop making temporary setbacks mean something about your worth. You stop interpreting discomfort as failure. You learn to stay—stay with your goals, your truth, your heart—even when things wobble.

And when you fall out of alignment (because you will), you know how to get back.

That is mastery.

FINAL THOUGHTS

Life after the shift isn't about becoming someone new. It's about becoming fully 'you'. The real you—the one who was always there beneath the old roles, fears, and masks.

It's not always loud or dramatic. But it's 'real'. It's free. And it's yours.

You don't have to earn it. Just stay with it. Return to it. Trust it.

Because now... you're living from the inside out.

A DAY IN LIFE AFTER THE SHIFT

Waking up after the shift feels different — not necessarily because every circumstance has changed, but because 'you' have. Instead of waking up with that gnawing sense of pressure or dread, there's a quiet calm. There's a knowing. You no longer leap out of bed trying to outrun failure or prove something to the world. You're not at war with your to-do list. You move into the day with clarity, a kind of internal rhythm that feels aligned.

You brush your teeth and, instead of berating yourself over what didn't get done yesterday, you feel a soft pride for having shown up — even in the smallest ways. There's space in your thoughts now. You dress not to impress, but to express. You speak more gently to yourself in the mirror. Your inner critic no longer has a microphone — it's still there, but you've stopped auditioning for its approval.

At work or in your business, you notice that problems feel more like puzzles than threats. You're more willing to delegate. You're less afraid of being misunderstood because your worth isn't hinged on being liked. You listen better. You lead more calmly. And when discomfort arises — which it always does — you face it instead of fleeing it. You ask, "What's this here to teach me?" rather than "How do I make it go away?"

At night, you sleep better — not because life is perfect, but because you're not dragging the emotional baggage of misalignment with you to bed. You're no longer trying to 'be' someone. You just 'are'. And that feels more than enough.

This is what a day feels like when the shift has taken root.

WHEN YOU SHIFT: WHO LEAVES, WHO STAYS, AND WHO'S NEW

One of the most surprising, and at times painful, consequences of inner alignment is that certain people no longer fit. It's not because you're better than them. It's because the contract that once bound you was signed by your old self — the one who needed their approval, played a certain role, or dimmed their light to keep the peace.

You may find that some friendships start to feel one-sided, or certain conversations feel hollow. The people you used to bend for no longer hold the same sway. This can be unsettling at first. You may worry: "Am I being selfish?" But what's really happening is that your nervous system is adjusting to a new baseline — one where authenticity trumps obligation.

Sometimes, it's family members who quietly distance themselves because your growth triggers their unspoken insecurities. Or longtime friends who lovingly (or not so lovingly) suggest you've "changed." And the truth is… you have. You no longer play the part they expect. The role you used to fill — the caretaker, the comic relief, the underachiever, the peacemaker — no longer defines you.

You may also attract new people — those whose energy matches your new inner truth. Relationships become less about mutual trauma bonding and more about mutual expansion. And this is one of the most rewarding outcomes of the shift: your outer world begins to reflect your inner reality.

Letting people go — or watching them fade from your life — can be bittersweet. Even when you know the shift is right, there's often a part of you that aches. That ache is the echo of the old self — the one who once believed connection had to be earned by shrinking, shape-shifting, or sacrificing. That version of you believed that acceptance had conditions.

But now... you know better.

You've stepped into a version of yourself that no longer begs for belonging — you *belong* to yourself first. You're not asking others to meet you halfway out of fear. You're standing firmly in your truth, your peace, your worth — and watching to see who can meet you there.

And then something beautiful and unexpected begins to happen:

The space that once felt empty starts to fill. And not with noise or drama or effort... but with people who see you *as you are*, and love you *because* of it.

These new connections feel different. They don't require performance or pretending. They feel easy, like deep exhales. Conversations nourish you. Time together energizes you. There's mutual respect, kindness, laughter that bubbles up without trying. These people may come from unexpected places — a new friend, a mentor, a colleague, even a romantic partner — but what they share in common is this: they are aligned with the version of you that's no longer hiding.

And here's something even more heartening:

Not *everyone* from your "before" chapter will fall away.

Some will surprise you.

Some of the very people you were afraid to lose will *rise* with you.

They'll notice the shift in you — the softness, the clarity, the quiet strength — and they'll be inspired by it. They'll listen more. Reflect more. Adjust their tone. Show up differently. Not because you demanded it, but because your transformation gave them permission to explore their own.

This is the quiet miracle of personal growth: sometimes, when you elevate, others elevate too.

Transformation doesn't always mean disconnection.

Sometimes, it brings people closer in ways you never imagined were possible.

And for those who don't come with you — for the friendships that quietly drift or the relationships that fade with grace — you'll find that the grief you expected is lighter than you feared. Because in its place is a growing sense of peace, power, and presence. You begin to understand that not all relationships are meant to last forever — but all of them taught you something.

And now you get to choose.

You get to build a circle that's based on truth, not survival.

Resonance, not obligation.

Connection, not coping.

And from here — life begins to feel fuller, lighter, richer.

Because *you're full of yourself in the best possible way.*

And the world responds to that truth with people who truly see you.

CHAPTER 18

TRIGGERS, TESTS & TRANSFORMATION

You've done the work. You've shifted your thoughts, your energy, and your vision of what's possible.

But, what if suddenly, life doesn't feel easier — it feels harder.

Things you thought were resolved begin to resurface. People start reacting differently to you. Unexpected obstacles appear. Doubt creeps in. It might seem like everything is falling apart... right after it finally started to come together.

But this isn't failure. It's initiation.

This is the part most people don't talk about: the part where your reality checks to see if you really mean it. If you'll hold the frequency of your new identity — even when old circumstances try to tempt you back.

Welcome to the phase of triggers and tests. It's not a punishment. It's proof you've moved.

THE ECHOES OF THE OLD SELF: UNDERSTANDING TRIGGERS

A "trigger" isn't just an emotional outburst. It's an echo — a reverberation from the past that gets activated when a familiar pattern is touched. You're not overreacting. You're responding from a part of you that remembers being small, powerless, afraid, or unseen.

Triggers often disguise themselves as logical reasons to backtrack:

- "Maybe I'm asking for too much."
- "I don't want to make things uncomfortable."
- "I should be grateful for what I already have."

But these thoughts are often the voice of your former self — the one who learned to play small to stay safe. When you're triggered, the subconscious is inviting you to regress. Not because it's malicious. But because it wants to protect you the only way it knows how — through patterns that kept you alive, even if not fulfilled.

THE TESTS: WHEN LIFE CHECKS YOUR ALIGNMENT

After a major internal shift, external life often responds with resistance. This is the test.

Tests are those moments when you're offered the chance to either:

- React the way you always did (and reinforce the old identity),
- Or respond from your new truth (and strengthen the shift).

Here's what that might look like:

- You raise your rates… and immediately lose a client. Test.
- You set a boundary… and someone calls you selfish. Test.
- You finally start your dream project… and your car breaks down. Test.
- You speak up confidently in a meeting… and someone talks over you. **Test.**

- You say "no" to something out of alignment… and feel instant guilt. **Test.**
- You finally launch your offer… and get crickets for the first week. **Test.**
- You choose rest over hustle… and someone accuses you of being lazy. **Test.**
- You decide to date with higher standards… and your phone goes silent. **Test.**
- You leave a toxic friendship… and feel a deep wave of loneliness. **Test.**
- You post something authentic online… and a relative criticizes it. **Test.**
- You invest in yourself for the first time… and an unexpected expense pops up. **Test.**
- You stop over-giving… and someone accuses you of being cold. **Test.**
- You take a leap toward your dream… and the people closest to you question it. **Test.**

These aren't coincidences. They're calibrations.

When you shift on the inside, the outer world temporarily lags behind — or challenges your new stance — to see if it's real. Not because the universe is cruel, but because manifestation is vibrational integrity. You must hold the new state "regardless of external evidence"… until external evidence matches it.

Transformation in Action: How to Pass the Test

Passing the test isn't about being perfect. It's about remembering.

Remembering that you're no longer operating from fear. That the identity you've claimed is more than a mindset — it's a standard. And like any standard, it gets tested to become stabilized.

Here's how to stay strong:

- **Breathe through the reaction.** - Triggers lose power when witnessed calmly.
- **Recognize the pattern.-** Say it out loud: "Ah, this is the old story trying to reclaim me."
- **Choose differently.-** Even if it's just in your thoughts. Choose to hold the new belief.
- **Remember**- you don't need to 'feel' ready to act in alignment. The act itself creates the feeling. And with each test passed, the identity becomes more automatic.

REFLECTION & REALIGNMENT: EXERCISES FOR INTEGRATION

Take time to reflect on these prompts. Write your answers. Let them guide your awareness.

- Where in my life do I feel "tested" right now?

- What patterns or reactions are trying to reclaim me?

- How does my old identity want me to respond — and how would my new

 identity respond instead?

- Who in my life is acting differently now that I've shifted?

- What would it look like to hold my new energy, even if no one else changes?

QUICK PRACTICE: GROUNDING IN THE NEW IDENTITY

When you feel triggered or tested, pause and place your hand over your heart. Speak your new identity aloud in the present tense: "I am _____." Repeat until your nervous system softens. This is your anchor.

YOU'RE NOT BEING PUNISHED — YOU'RE BEING INITIATED

The journey of transformation isn't just about achieving goals. It's about becoming the version of you who naturally attracts and sustains them.

Triggers and tests are not setbacks. They're confirmations.

They're life saying, "Let's see if this change is real." And when you respond from your new alignment, something extraordinary happens: you don't just maintain the shift — you deepen it.

You move from "having" a new identity… to "being" it.

So don't fear the test. Don't run from the trigger. Welcome them. Each one is a doorway.

Because if you can stand in your truth when it's hard, you'll never lose it when it's easy.

This is how transformation becomes permanent. This is how your new life becomes your only life.

You're not going back.

You're being initiated forward.

REFLECTION: THE TEST IS NOT THE PROBLEM

Tests don't show up to block your path. They show up to **anchor your new identity.**

The old version of you had rehearsed reactions. These tests simply give you the chance to choose differently. To practice being the version of you that doesn't abandon yourself.

LET'S TAKE A MOMENT TO REFLECT:

- Where in your life are you being tested right now?
- What reaction are you tempted to give — and what identity would that reinforce?
- What would your *aligned* response look like instead?
- How would it feel to choose your new truth... even if no one else applauds it?

NOW ASK YOURSELF:

"What am I proving to myself in this moment?"

Because you're not here to pass someone else's test.

You're here to pass your own.

And once you begin recognizing your triggers and rising to the tests, something subtle but powerful begins to happen: you're no longer just reacting to life—you're consciously shaping it. And with that shift comes a new opportunity: to fully embody the version of you that has already arrived.

VISUALIZATION: STEPPING INTO THE SHIFT

Take a moment. Breathe deeply.

Now imagine yourself, not in the process of becoming—but already living from your shift.

You're walking through your day as the version of you who no longer second-guesses, who no longer apologizes for your needs, your dreams, or your light. What does that feel like in your body? Is there more space? More breath?

Visualize how you speak. How you walk into a room. How you respond to challenge.

Picture the types of people around you—those who now reflect your deeper truth, not your former fears. Are they supportive? Are they strong? Are they peaceful? Let yourself feel them beside you, as if they've always been there.

Now notice your inner voice. It no longer whispers warnings or self-doubt. It's calm. Grounded. Encouraging. A quiet confidence pulses beneath your every choice.

You've stopped rehearsing failure. You're now preparing for fulfillment.

This visualization isn't fantasy—it's a frequency shift. The more time you spend in it, the more real it becomes. And soon, this version of you won't be something you're imagining… it will be the life you're inhabiting.

You've done the work. You've seen what was hidden. You've passed the tests and turned the triggers into turning points.

Now… this is the reward.

The shift has happened.

The rest is simply remembering who you now are.

WHO ARE YOU BECOMING — EVEN WHEN OTHERS DON'T APPROVE?

Take a moment to think about the last time someone responded *negatively* to your growth.

Did they question your decision?

Mock your ambition?

Pull away emotionally or energetically?

Now ask yourself:

- Were they reacting to *you*... or to the version of you they were most comfortable with?
- What did that interaction stir in you — guilt? Doubt? The urge to explain or justify?
- What old identity were you being invited to step back into?

Often, the *real* test isn't about setting the boundary — it's about sitting in the silence after.

The stillness. The discomfort. The unknown.

That's where transformation happens — not in the action, but in your willingness to *stay aligned* after you've made it.

Example:

You decide to prioritize your well-being and decline a family obligation for the first time in years.

They say: "You've changed."

You want to explain, soften it, take it back.

But instead, you pause. You breathe. You *stay*.

And in that moment, something shifts.

You realize the discomfort is not a signal to go backward — it's a sign you're moving forward.

Finally raise your rates to reflect your value — and your longest client says they "can't afford you anymore."

- → Old identity: *The people-pleaser who avoids discomfort to stay liked.*
- → Test: Do you lower your rates to keep them, or trust that you're making space for higher alignment?
- You launch your new offer with confidence, but sales are slow at first.
- → Old identity: *The self-doubter who needs immediate validation to feel safe.*
- → Test: Do you panic and pivot too soon, or trust the foundation you've laid?
- You choose to delegate work you used to control completely — and your team struggles a little at first.
- → Old identity: *The over-functioner who needs to feel essential to feel worthy.*
- → Test: Do you jump back in to "fix" it, or lead from trust and long-term vision?
- You set a boundary with a friend who's constantly negative — and they stop calling.

- → Old identity: *The emotional caretaker who absorbs others' feelings to feel valuable.*
- → Test: Do you chase after them, or allow the silence to clarify the relationship?
- You start eating healthier and skipping the nightly wine — and your partner teases you about "being too good now."
- → Old identity: *The conformer who downplays change to stay relatable.*
- → Test: Do you shrink your progress to fit in, or proudly continue anyway?
- You start speaking up more in your family — and someone jokes, "Who do you think you are?"
- → Old identity: *The quiet one who avoids attention to avoid judgment.*
- → Test: Do you laugh it off and go quiet again, or keep expressing your truth?

CHAPTER 19

YOUR SUCCESS SET POINT — AND HOW TO RAISE IT

Have you ever noticed a pattern in your life where things are going incredibly well—your business is thriving, your relationships feel aligned, your energy is high—and then, almost like clockwork, something derails it? A fight with a partner. An unexpected expense. A wave of procrastination. Or even an unexplained sense of guilt or discomfort.

It's not always external forces at play. Sometimes, it's your internal thermostat doing exactly what it was trained to do—bring you back to the emotional temperature you're most familiar with.

Imagine you hear a loud knock at your front door. You glance out the window and see a face you don't recognize. Would you swing the door open wide to a complete stranger? Probably not. Most people hesitate — maybe crack the door open just an inch, cautious and uncertain. But if it were a familiar friend standing there, you wouldn't think twice. You'd welcome them in with ease.

The same is true when it comes to stepping into a new set point. At first, it feels unfamiliar — even uncomfortable. You might only allow yourself to try it out in small ways, just enough to test the waters. But as you get to know this new version of yourself — the one aligned with your highest potential — you begin to feel more at ease. Bit by bit, the door opens wider. Trust builds. And eventually, what once felt foreign begins to feel like home.

This is the natural process of transformation: cautious at first, but increasingly powerful as you recognize that the person knocking is actually *you* — the real you, finally coming into a new set point.

WHAT IS A SUCCESS SET POINT?

Your success set point is your subconscious comfort zone for how much joy, wealth, love, recognition, or ease you feel emotionally safe experiencing. It's the ceiling your nervous system was trained to maintain, even if your conscious mind is aiming for more.

You can think of it like a thermostat in your home. If your internal setting says you're only allowed 70 degrees of joy, and suddenly life heats up to 85 with a big win—your subconscious system will "cool things down" to regulate what feels safe.

WHY WE SABOTAGE 'THE GOOD'

At first glance, this might seem confusing. Why would anyone sabotage more love, abundance, or happiness?

The subconscious recorded warnings. And now, when you approach similar highs in your own life, your body interprets them as danger zones. Cue the sabotage—usually in the form of stress, distraction, self-doubt, or conflict.

SIGNS YOU'VE HIT YOUR INTERNAL CEILING

Here are some common signs you've bumped up against your current success set point:

- You experience a major win... and immediately feel anxious or uncomfortable.
- You get a promotion... and start procrastinating on projects.
- You finally meet a kind, available partner... and suddenly lose interest.
- You receive more money than usual... and find ways to spend it fast.
- Things are going well... and you pick a fight or create chaos.

These aren't flaws. They're clues. Indicators that you're expanding beyond what your emotional system has learned to hold.

YOUR EMOTIONAL CAPACITY

This chapter isn't just about identifying what limits you. It's about building your capacity to receive and 'hold' more—without collapsing, sabotaging, or numbing out.

Just like physical muscles grow with consistent training, your emotional capacity expands through gentle, repeated exposure to the very things you're not used to having.

Receiving more love. More praise. More peace. More money. More rest.

At first, these can feel unfamiliar—even triggering. That's okay. **The goal isn't to be fearless. It's to become tolerant of the goodness you once pushed away.**

REFLECTION: WHERE'S YOUR SET POINT NOW?

Take a moment and think about each area of your life. Use these prompts to discover your current emotional ceiling:

1. **Money** - What's the most money you've ever comfortably held without spending or giving it away? Do you feel guilt or fear with more financial success?
2. **Visibility** - How do you feel when people praise you or acknowledge your gifts? Do you find yourself downplaying your wins?
3. **Love and Relationships** - How much intimacy and connection feels safe for you? Do you pull away when someone gets too close?
4. **Success and Ease** - Do you believe you have to hustle or suffer to earn your success? What happens when things come easily to you?

Your honest answers will reveal the limits you're working within—not to shame you, but to help you gently expand.

HOW TO RAISE YOUR SUCCESS SET POINT (WITHOUT TRIGGERING SABOTAGE)

1. Normalize the New

Exposure rewires safety. The more often you experience a new level of success or joy, the less foreign—and threatening—it becomes. Start small.

If receiving compliments feels hard, practice saying "thank you" without deflecting.

If resting triggers guilt, start with short pauses.

If visibility scares you, post something meaningful once a week.

Each time you stay with the good, even just a little longer than you used to, you raise your set point.

2. Expand Your Nervous System's Capacity –

Success doesn't just require mindset shifts—it requires 'body shifts'.

Practice grounding techniques like breathwork, somatic exercises, or even gentle movement to help your body stay present with new levels of goodness.

Create rituals to remind your system it's safe to feel joy, ease, and expansion.

3. Update the Old Story

Find the origin of your old set point. Was it "People like us don't get rich"? "Love always leads to pain"? "If I'm seen, I'll be attacked"?

Once you spot the story, you can write a new one:

- "People like me are allowed to thrive."
- "Love can be both deep and safe."
- "Being seen is how I change lives."

4. Celebrate and Integrate

Celebrate progress—especially the subtle, internal kind.

Not every win is flashy. Sometimes the real breakthrough is staying calm after receiving praise, or noticing your desire to run—but choosing to stay.

Let your wins land. Let them settle. Let them become normal.

THE TRUTH ABOUT EXPANSION

Expanding your success set point isn't about constantly reaching for more. It's about learning to 'hold' more of what you truly want.

It's about letting joy, wealth, peace, and intimacy become your new baseline—not fleeting highs followed by emotional crashes. You were never meant to touch success and then retreat.

You were meant to live there.

And you can.

CHAPTER 20

SEEING THE INVISIBLE — UNDERSTANDING OTHERS THROUGH THE LENS OF HIDDEN PATTERNS

Seeing the Invisible — Understanding Others Through the Lens of Hidden Patterns

You're doing deep work. You're uncovered your hidden goals. You're shifting the sabotaging patterns that once ruled your life from the shadows. And now, something even more profound happens you start to see those same patterns operating in others.

This isn't about judging or labeling people. It's about understanding.

It's the moment when your inner work becomes your outer lens — not to critique the world, but to connect with it more consciously.

WHY PEOPLE BEHAVE THE WAY THEY DO

Think of the people in your life. Some over-apologize. Some brag. Some self-sabotage just when things get good. Others can't seem to tolerate peace, so they stir up drama.

Now, instead of being frustrated or confused by these behaviors, imagine being able to *see* the deeper pattern underneath. To sense what their subconscious might be protecting — the identity they had to shape to feel safe or seen.

You no longer take things so personally. You no longer get caught in an emotional crossfire. You're not excusing bad behavior, but you are able to decode it — and that changes everything.

Because when you understand where someone's actions are coming from, it opens the door to compassion.

You recognize the over-explainer isn't annoying — they're trying to prove they deserve to exist.

The avoidant friend isn't flaky — they're scared of disappointing you.

The partner who resists commitment? Maybe they were raised to believe love always costs your freedom.

EMOTIONAL INTELLIGENCE, EVOLVED

This kind of insight is a hallmark of true emotional intelligence. But it's more than that — it's *energetic intelligence*. It's the ability to feel what's going unspoken. To perceive the old patterns beneath polished personas.

And once you see it, you can't unsee it.

You hear a friend dismiss their own success with a joke — and you notice the buried guilt.

You see a coworker sabotage a promotion — and you intuit the fear of outgrowing their social circle.

You spot a relative's chronic criticism — and recognize it as their way of keeping people close (because praise, to them, means vulnerability).

The more you tune into this layer of reality, the more connected — and clear — your relationships become.

COMMUNICATION SHIFTS INSTANTLY

When you see the hidden goal in others, your words change. Your tone softens. You ask better questions. You listen between the lines.

You stop needing to win arguments and start creating space for growth.

You realize that pushing people doesn't help them evolve — *seeing* them does.

Imagine a conversation where someone lashes out and, instead of reacting, you pause and wonder: "What are they trying to protect right now?"

That moment of reflection doesn't just calm you — it creates a shift in the energy of the exchange. Because instead of escalating, you're offering presence.

And presence is powerful.

Boundaries Become Easier

Paradoxically, this deeper understanding also makes it easier to set boundaries.

When you know someone's behavior is coming from a pattern — not from you — it's easier to say, "I care about you, but this isn't okay," without guilt.

You don't need to demonize them to protect yourself.

You simply stand in your new identity, hold your emotional center, and choose what you'll allow in your space.

And sometimes, with this new perspective, even difficult relationships begin to shift. Not because you forced them — but because your presence invited a new kind of interaction.

It Makes You a Leader in Any Room

Whether you're running a business, raising a family, or navigating friendships, this ability changes how you lead.

People feel safer around someone who isn't easily thrown off.

They trust someone who sees past the surface and holds space without judgment.

You become someone others can confide in — because you're not reacting from your wounds, you're listening from your awareness.

This doesn't mean you're never triggered or always perfect. It means you're now equipped with the tools and insight to navigate relationships in a way that brings more truth, peace, and connection.

A GIFT TO THE WORLD

Your healing doesn't stop with you.

When you do this kind of work, you create a ripple effect. Every time you choose understanding over reactivity, presence over projection, awareness over assumption — you model what's possible.

You become a mirror in which others can begin to see themselves more clearly, more compassionately.

And that, perhaps, is the greatest gift of all.

THE BIGGER PICTURE: FROM PERSONAL INSIGHT TO GLOBAL IMPACT

What would happen if more people — especially those in positions of power — understood their own hidden goals?

Imagine political leaders aware of their emotional triggers. CEOs who didn't overcompensate for childhood wounds. **Public figures who didn't mistake control for confidence or dominance for strength.**

We live in a world shaped by the subconscious patterns of those who've never examined them. Entire nations are sometimes guided by leaders still reacting to old fears — the fear of not being respected, the fear of losing power, the fear of appearing weak.

When you understand this, the world stops feeling like chaos and starts to feel... tragically familiar.

Because you recognize it. You've seen it in yourself.

The overreaching government that can't stop tightening its grip? It's the same as the individual who micromanages everything out of fear of losing control.

The culture that devalues vulnerability? It mirrors the person who hides their pain behind sarcasm or workaholism.

When leaders (and citizens) operate from **unexamined fears, it creates policies, conflicts, and social norms rooted in unconscious survival — not conscious creation.**

But just like in your personal life... awareness changes everything.

CONVERSATIONS THAT COULD CHANGE THE WORLD

Think of how many global challenges could be approached differently if more people understood the hidden goals shaping behavior.

Diplomatic standstills could be softened by seeing the emotional needs beneath the posturing.

Social divides could be bridged not by blame, but by deep listening to generational pain.

Even within nations, political parties could begin to recognize how their messaging—and their resistance—is often rooted in fear: fear of losing tradition, fear of irrelevance, fear of being misunderstood.

This doesn't mean we should excuse harmful actions. But it does mean we should **become skilled at recognizing what fuels them — because only then can we change the fuel source.**

And it begins with us.

Every time you engage in a difficult conversation and **choose curiosity over condemnation, you are rehearsing a better world.**

Every time you pause before reacting—and instead ask, "What are they protecting right now?" — you are de-escalating, disarming, and inviting truth to the surface.

This is how personal growth becomes global contribution.

INNER EVOLUTION CREATES OUTER REVOLUTION

The great lie of our time is that real power lies in force or strategy. But history—and healing—shows us that the deepest shifts come not from dominance, but from transformation.

And transformation starts inside.

You may never stand at a podium or sit at a peace summit. **But when you embody emotional mastery, you influence every room you walk into. And that influence ripples.**

A healed person raises children differently.

A conscious leader makes decisions differently.

A present partner loves differently.

And all of it matters. Deeply.

Because the world we long to live in — one with less conflict, more connection, and greater compassion — *is built by people who've dared to do the inner work.*

So don't underestimate what you're doing here. Don't minimize your journey.

You're not just changing your life.

You're **contributing to a new blueprint for human interaction** — one where we stop projecting our unhealed wounds onto others and start building from wholeness instead.

BEYOND PERSONAL: SHAPING THE WORLD WITH EMOTIONAL INSIGHT

Imagine what our world might look like if more leaders — in government, business, education, or media — understood the hidden motivations driving human behavior. Not just surface-level psychology, but the deeper emotional patterns that form in childhood and echo through adulthood, influencing decisions, alliances, reactions, and even wars.

So many public conflicts, both national and international, are built not only on ideologies but on identities — unexamined, inherited, and fiercely protected. Leaders carry their own internal saboteurs, often masked by ego, rhetoric, or power. They may lash out not because of rational strategy, but because an old, unhealed wound has been activated. A need to win. A fear of not being seen. A subconscious drive to prove something that has nothing to do with the present moment.

When these internal patterns go unchecked, they show up in policies, negotiations, and press conferences — often with devastating consequences.

But what if more leaders learned to pause?

What if, in moments of tension, they knew to ask:

- "What fear might be hiding under this reaction?"
- "Am I responding to this situation… or to something from long ago?"
- "Is this about progress — or about protecting an old version of myself?"

The ability to **reflect instead of react** could change everything.

Because when a leader understands their own patterns, they also become better at recognizing others' motivations — including adversaries'. Instead of escalating every conflict into a power struggle, they may begin to decode what the other side *isn't* saying… and what old fear may be shaping the behavior.

This doesn't mean excusing harmful actions or avoiding accountability. But it does mean learning to lead with clarity, not reactivity. With presence, not projection. With purpose, not protection.

This level of awareness is rare — but it's not unreachable.

In fact, it starts with you.

As more individuals learn to see and **shift their hidden patterns, the ripple effect expands.** Relationships transform. Communities soften. Teams operate with more synergy. And **yes, entire countries could change... simply because someone in power learned to pause, reflect, and realign.**

It may sound idealistic — but it's also deeply practical. **Emotional intelligence isn't just a soft skill. It's a stabilizing force.** And in a world that often feels divided and reactive, this kind of internal grounding might be one of the most advanced tools we have for peace, progress, and possibility.

REAL-WORLD REFLECTIONS: FROM BOARDROOMS TO DIPLOMATIC TABLES

We've seen glimpses of this kind of emotional leadership in the real world.

When **Nelson Mandela stepped out of prison after 27 years and chose reconciliation over retaliation,** he wasn't just making a political move — he was embodying a **profound emotional shift**. He understood that reacting from pain would perpetuate the cycle of suffering. Instead, he chose a higher pattern. One that rewrote the narrative not only for South Africa, but for the world.

Or consider **Barack Obama, whose presidency was marked not only by historic milestones but also by unprecedented levels of scrutiny,** resistance, and personal attacks — Despite the vitriol often aimed at him, **he maintained a remarkable sense of composure, dignity, and emotional maturity**. He didn't match outrage with outrage. Instead, he responded with thoughtfulness, restraint, and a **steadfast commitment to unity.**

Whether addressing the nation after heartbreaking tragedies — like the Charleston church shooting, — or navigating global tensions with diplomacy over aggression, Obama exemplified a leadership style rooted in inner calm. **His emotional regulation became a quiet superpower.** He showed the world that strength isn't about who can shout the loudest — it's about who can stay grounded, clear, **and humane when the stakes are highest**.

In a time when divisiveness often dominates, **his presidency remains a powerful example of how grace under fire can be a transformative form of leadership.**

Or take **Jacinda Ardern, former Prime Minister of New Zealand**, who consistently demonstrated emotional clarity and compassion during times of crisis — from terror attacks to the COVID-19 pandemic. Her calm, human-centered leadership reminded people that **strength doesn't always roar. Sometimes, it simply listens.**

These leaders didn't escape pain or pressure. But **they didn't let the past dictate their choices. They reflected, then responded**. And by doing so, they elevated everyone around them.

Now imagine bringing that kind of awareness into your own circles — your family, your workplace, your community.

TRY THIS: REFLECTION FOR RELATIONAL MASTERY

Use these prompts to expand your empathy and sharpen your insight into the people around you:

- Think of someone who frustrates you. What role might *they* have learned to play in childhood?

- What does this role help them avoid or protect?
- When you feel reactive toward them, what part of *your* old identity might be getting triggered?
- Can you see past their behavior and connect with the fear or pattern beneath it?
- What could change in the relationship if you responded from your healed self — instead of your hurt self?

This is not about excusing poor behavior. It's about understanding it, so you can choose your next move with greater power and peace.

The more we learn to see through this lens, the more clarity we bring to every conversation. **And in doing so, we become part of the solution — not just in our personal lives, but in the world at large.**

FINAL THOUGHT

Emotional intelligence isn't only about self-awareness. It's also about systemic impact. **It's how the ripple of one healed pattern can travel across a dinner table, a team, a city, even a global negotiation.**

You may never hold political office or run a company — **but your ability to model grounded, emotionally intelligent behavior is leadership of the highest form.**

And the world is watching.

You've just begun a powerful journey — one that isn't just teaching you how to set better goals, but how to uncover the *real reasons* you haven't already achieved them. **The ideas in this book aren't** *surface-level strategies. **They reach beneath the obvious, into the unconscious patterns** that quietly direct so much of our lives.*

And now... you see them.

You're exploring how childhood roles shaped your adult behavior. **You're identifying how the mind will do almost anything to protect you from feeling disconnected**, even at the cost of your success. And most importantly, you're learning how to bring those patterns into the light — so they no longer run the show from the shadows.

That alone is life changing.

But it doesn't stop with you.

Once you understand the hidden saboteurs — and the deep, human reasons behind them — you start to **see them in others**. In your partner. In your friends. In your family. Even in the people you've struggled to connect with.

Suddenly, what used to feel like **resistance or rejection becomes something else: recognition**. You begin to understand their patterns the way you've learned to understand your own. And from that place, you create deeper connection, not conflict. Compassion, not condemnation. **Harmony, not hostility.**

This work doesn't just unlock success.

It brings you home to yourself — the real you, underneath the roles, the rules, and the resistance. The you that's been waiting all along.

And from here, everything becomes possible.

You've now uncovered what many have not and may never— the invisible tug-of-war between the life you want and the hidden programming that's been holding you back.

CONCLUSION

WALKING FORWARD WITH CLARITY

While at the end of the book, you're not ending a journey—you're stepping into a deeper one. The work you're doing here **isn't simply intellectual; it's foundational.** You've been peeling back the layers, examining the patterns, and confronting the quiet contracts you didn't even know you signed.

You're naming your hidden goals. You're rewriting the script. You're aligning your intentions with your truth. And most importantly, you're returning to the awareness that you hold the pen—that your life story is still unfolding, and you are **no longer writing from fear, but from clarity.**

This work doesn't guarantee a smooth path. It ensures an 'authentic' one. And with that authenticity comes a sense of peace that no external accomplishment can replicate. When your internal compass is aligned, your decisions will come from wisdom, not worry. **Your actions will come from purpose, not pressure.**

The tug-of-war may not disappear entirely—old habits, fears, and doubts don't vanish overnight. But now you have the tools to meet them with grace. You'll notice them faster. Realign quicker.

And choose more powerfully. That's what mastery looks like: **not perfection, but presence.**

If there's one message to take with you, let it be this: **You're not behind. You're not broken. You're not late. You're right on time— and you're more powerful than you've been led to believe.**

From here, every step forward is different — because it's no longer guided by fear, but by truth.

You are no longer living by the role you were assigned.

You're now writing your own story.

So, this is not goodbye. It's a hand on your shoulder, a reminder in your pocket, a whisper in your future moments of doubt: You had the power all along. And now, it's yours to live by.

YOU DON'T HAVE TO DO THIS ALONE

Ready to continue the journey?

Transformation doesn't end with the final page. In fact, this is where the real integration begins. And you don't have to navigate it alone.

If you're ready to go deeper, stay accountable, and continue evolving in a supportive, high-vibration environment — classes, coaching, and group programs are available to help you bring this work fully to life.

Whether you're looking for one-on-one clarity, guided implementation of the Goal Magnet framework, or a like-minded community that truly *gets it* — the next step is waiting for you.

Explore available options:

- Live or virtual classes to deepen your breakthrough
- Personalized coaching to target your specific blocks
- Private groups for ongoing connection, momentum, and inspiration

You've done incredible work. Now you can join others and take the journey together.

To learn more or join the next group, visit: ***www.success-411.com***

You're not starting over — you're rising higher. And this time, with real support behind you.

The 'One Goal Workbook' is your hands-on companion to this book. It offers step-by-step exercises, reflection prompts, and guided practices to help you uncover, shift, and realign your hidden goals in real-time.

Whether you're a visual learner, someone who processes best by writing things out, or you simply want to see these principles in action in your own life—this workbook is the perfect next move.

To order your copy and begin the hands-on process of aligning your subconscious beliefs with your conscious goals — through exercises, reflections, and powerful reprogramming techniques — visit www.success-411.com **This is where your transformation becomes tangible.**

ABOUT THE AUTHOR

Mona Thorpe is a sought-after Manifestation Coach with more than 30 years of experience guiding clients to uncover and transform the subconscious barriers that sabotage success. Her work goes far beyond surface-level affirmations—she helps clients align their internal programming with the goals they most want to achieve, creating sustainable breakthroughs in both personal and professional life.

Her clients include high-performing entrepreneurs, executives, and creatives—individuals starting out on their transformational journey or who have achieved much, yet feel something vital is still just out of reach. Mona's signature process empowers them to identify the hidden inner conflicts that drain momentum and rewire their mindset for lasting success.

In addition to her coaching work, Mona is a successful serial entrepreneur. Her ventures have earned recognition in Oprah's Favorite Things, features in The New York Times, and leadership roles in executive search for top-level professionals. This real-world business acumen gives her a grounded, results-oriented edge—making her a rare blend of intuitive coach and accomplished businesswoman.

What fuels her mission is deeply personal: a challenging childhood that sparked her commitment to rewrite her own narrative—and help others do the same. Today,

Mona is dedicated to showing others how to harness the true power of alignment, so they can live with purpose, freedom, and the joy of being in full control of their success story.

To explore more of Mona's work or inquire about coaching events, visit www.success-411.com or email her directly mthorpe@success-411.com

ACKNOWLEDGMENTS

To those who've walked this journey with me—clients, colleagues, friends, and family—your presence has been more than support; it has been a living reminder of the power of growth, truth, and alignment.

To my clients, whose courage to face their hidden blocks and rewrite their inner stories inspired the heart of this book—thank you for trusting me. Your breakthroughs have shaped this work more than you know.

To the mentors and thought leaders who came before—thank you for lighting the path and challenging conventional thinking.

To those who doubted or challenged me along the way—thank you, too. Your resistance sharpened my clarity and deepened my resolve.

And finally, to the reader: thank you for doing the work, for being curious, for choosing alignment. My hope is that this book continues to serve you every time you return to it. May your journey be rich, real, and deeply yours.

"You're not behind. You're not broken. You're not late. You're right on time—and you're more powerful than you've been led to believe."

"Keep walking forward. Keep aligning. **Your life is not waiting—it's responding**."

www.ingramcontent.com/pod-product-compliance
Lightning Source LLC
Chambersburg PA
CBHW060511100426
42743CB00009B/1284